WHAT PEOPLE ARE SAYING ABOUT

PAGAN PORT[...]IC

It would be easy to sa[...]ook for beginners – but Lucya St[...] packs so much information into 25,000 words that it qualifies as a 'must-have' introduction to the fascinating subject of candle magic. I particularly like the down-to-earth, chatty approach that reads like a casual conversation around the kitchen table – by candle light, of course. Candle magic is one of the simplest, yet one of the oldest, most powerful forms of spell-casting and an essential addition to any witch's toolbox of tricks – so if you want to discover more about the glittering, shimmering, flickering, dancing world of candle magic then this is the book for you.

Mélusine Draco, Principal of Coven of the Scales and author of the *Traditional Witchcraft* series of books

In this book, Lucya Starza gives us good practical advice about working ordinary everyday magic using a part of our normal life – the candle. It is a comprehensive guide on how to use candles for spells, in rituals and for meditation and divination. It has quickly become my preferred book for all aspects of candle magic.

Philip Heselton, author of *Witchfather: A Life of Gerald Gardner, Gerald Gardner and the Cauldron of Inspiration* and *Wiccan Roots: Gerald Gardner and the Modern Witchcraft Revival*

I have absolute faith in the efficacy of Lucya's candle magic, which was a great help to me during a crisis.

Caroline Wise, member of the steering body of The Fellowship of Isis and author of *Finding Elen: The Quest for Elen of the Ways*

Pagan Portals: Candle Magic is my favourite type of 'how to' book. There are no presumptions about the experience level of the reader, which means everyone, from the novice to the journeyman, can pick up this book and not only enjoy the style and humour of Lucya's writing, but definitely learn something practical and useful. Lucya guides the reader through magical exercises, focusing on 'learning through doing', but with enough theory and background to make the exercises engaging and thought provoking, and very effective! The level of detail makes the subject fascinating and enthralling, and her passion and skill for candle magic shines through her words. An immensely useful book for anyone interested in candle magic or spell work. This book is joining the select few 'well thumbed' volumes on my shelf that I refer back to again and again.

Mabh Savage, author of *A Modern Celt: Seeking the Ancestors*

Pagan Portals
Candle Magic

A Witch's Guide to Spells and Rituals

Pagan Portals
Candle Magic

A Witch's Guide to Spells and Rituals

Lucya Starza

MOON
BOOKS

Winchester, UK
Washington, USA

First published by Moon Books, 2016
Moon Books is an imprint of John Hunt Publishing Ltd., Laurel House, Station Approach,
Alresford, Hants, SO24 9JH, UK
office1@jhpbooks.net
www.johnhuntpublishing.com
www.moon-books.net

For distributor details and how to order please visit the 'Ordering' section on our website.

Text copyright: Lucya Starza 2015

ISBN: 978 1 78535 043 6
Library of Congress Control Number: 2015953278

A CIP catalogue record for this book is available from the British Library.

Design: Lee Nash

Printed and bound by CPI Group (UK) Ltd, Croydon, CR0 4YY, UK

We operate a distinctive and ethical publishing philosophy in all
areas of our business, from our global network of authors to
production and worldwide distribution.

CONTENTS

This book is dedicated to my beloved husband John and to all my wonderful friends. In particular, Liz and Stephen – I could not have finished this book without you.

Introduction

Candle magic is fun and easy. I've been doing candle magic since I was a toddler – and I expect you have too. Every birthday I looked forward to making a wish over the candles on a big, exciting cake.

As with all spells, there was a little ritual to be performed: one candle for every year; the wish could not be spoken out loud, because wishes shared might not come true; finally, all the candles had to be blown out in a single breath – increasingly hard to do as the years went by.

Did my wishes come true? Maybe. To be honest, I can't remember even one thing I wished for. But there was another type of candle magic that did work – that was the tiny flame on a little candle in my bedroom that kept bad dreams at bay. It was the first circle of protection I knew. It warded against ghoulies and ghosties and things that went bump in the night. It worked. With that candle lit, I knew no fairy-tale monster could get me and I slept like a baby...

Nowadays, no one would consider it safe to leave a lit candle in any bedroom while the inhabitants slept, let alone in a child's room. But, back when I was young, what we now call tea-lights were called night-lights and they were specifically intended to help babies sleep without fear. You can still get lights that do that, but they are electric and considerably safer than naked flames. Times change and safety is vital.

In magic, as in fairy tales, things often come in threes. Here is my third childhood tale of a candle ritual.

My family attended a Catholic church on Sundays. My favourite spot was where votive candles flickered on a large, wrought-iron stand in front of the statue of Mary with the baby Jesus. I loved to watch the rows of little flames, knowing that as they burned down the silent petitions of those who lit them were heard by Our Lady. Catholics do not call her a goddess, let alone the Goddess, but to me she is an aspect of the divine feminine. In times of need, I still light a candle to the Goddess, Our Mother, Who Art in Heaven – and anywhere else she wants to be – and feel her comfort in the warm glow.

What is amazing about candles is that even for adults they seem to exude enchantment. A meal for two becomes a romantic dinner by the light of a candle; a bathroom becomes a place for deep relaxation if you place candles around the edge of the tub; scented candles can fill our living spaces with whatever mood we want to create more effectively than spraying an atomiser. Ghost stories should always be read by candlelight...

For the past 30 years I have been a Pagan and a witch. Most witchcraft rituals that take place after dark are lit by candles. The soft glow helps transport us outside normal space and time to a liminal place where all things are possible – and that is the best place for magic to work. Candles are also an essential ingredient for many spells, even ones not specifically labelled as candle magic.

In this book I am going to share with you my knowledge of candle spells and rituals along with useful hints and tips and a few secrets too. This book is about how to harness the magic of candles in many different ways. I hope you enjoy it, and that it helps your wishes all come true.

One

Candle Spells

First Steps in Candle Magic

A Simple Candle Spell

If you're reading this book, I'm guessing you want to do some candle spells, so I'll leave the history, theory and safety advice until later. Let's start with some practical magic.

Go and find yourself a tea-light candle; an ordinary white one will be fine. Most people have one or two somewhere around the house, even if that's just in case of a power cut. Obviously if you are reading this book on the bus, in the library or sneakily beside the shelf in a shop, you will probably have to wait until you get home to find a candle, but do it as soon as you can. The best way to learn magic is by doing it – not just reading books.

Once you have a candle, find something to scratch a word onto the wax – a small craft knife will do, or a pen knife. If you are an experienced witch you might have a special knife set aside for this kind of thing (sometimes called a boline if you want to get technical). Or you could use a cocktail stick or toothpick. Any of these will do just fine.

Now think of something you want to wish for. Keep it simple and try to sum it up in one word; *health, wealth, happiness, love, success, security, justice* are all good words to use. Take the tea-light out of its casing and scratch that word onto the side or bottom. If you want a new job or a new home, just scratch 'job' or 'home'. Short and simple is best.

While you are inscribing your word, concentrate on a mental picture of what your life will be like when your wish comes true. (This technique is called 'visualisation' and it draws on the powers of the imagination to help you see clearly what you want and work towards getting it – but that's enough theory for now.) Hold the candle in your hands for a moment or two after you have finished carving your wish, but continue the visualisation.

Find something safe to put the tea-light in. If you have a

3

pretty tea-light holder, that's ideal, but you can put it in a glass or ceramic dish or a jam jar – or a cauldron if you've got one. (I find cauldrons are better as candle holders than as things to brew potions in – I usually use a saucepan for potion brewing, but I'm digressing.) Light the candle. Ideally, let it burn down all in one go, but that isn't always practical and you shouldn't leave a lit candle unattended. An alternative is to burn the candle over several evenings until it is finished.

One final bit of advice – don't keep wondering whether your spell will work. When you aren't actually doing the spell, try to keep it out of your thoughts. Carry on with your normal life and let the magic happen. If you keep worrying about whether your wish will come true there's a chance you will disperse the magic through fretting about it.

Looking Ahead

Now you've done a candle spell. You may be thinking that if it works, why do you need to read a whole book on the subject? Well, many experienced witches only ever use candle magic in this basic form. Simple spells can be very effective, just as simple food may be what we prepare most often out of choice. But, as with cookery, there's a lot more you can do beyond the basics.

These early chapters are the best place to start if you are new to witchcraft and magic. The book starts simply and gradually goes deeper. There are all sorts of ways you can make your candle magic more effective – through different colours and scents, by the powers of different phases of the Moon and days of the week and by adding all sorts of other witchy ingredients into the mix. I promise you won't have to add any wing of bat or eye of newt to your candle spells though – at least not real ones. I have used some bat-shaped candles in the past.

As well as covering more complex spells and candle rituals, I'll briefly explain how to make candles. Oh and I'll also be covering a bit of history and theory for those who like that kind of thing. And if you're a witch who has been doing candle magic for years, I hope I'll still be able to teach you one or two new things.

Types of Candle

Pretty much any candle can be used for magic, but different types are better for different things. I made a classic mistake when I first cast a candle spell. I picked a big, impressive candle, carved my intention down the side, lit it and waited for it to burn down.

The instructions I had read for the spell told me I had to let it burn all in one go, so that was what I did. After I got bored staring at it, I carried the ruddy thing around the house while I did the housework, cooked supper, ate, watched a movie on the telly and stayed up long past the witching hour reading a book. The candle was still only half burnt. The lesson I learnt was: next time get a smaller candle.

Now I am a wise enough witch to know you don't always have to let a candle burn down at one sitting for a spell to work, but it is best to use the right type of candle for the spell you want to cast. Here are various types of candle you are likely to find and a bit about the spells and rituals they are best for.

Tea-Lights and Night-Lights

The most versatile and common candles, tea-lights can be used pretty much whenever and wherever you want – the dining table, bathroom, garden, bedroom, meditation space or altar. Every witch should keep a stock. To state the obvious, tea-lights are small wax discs about 1cm to 2cm high and about 4cm wide. They are usually encased in a metal, plastic or wax-paper case and have a central wick with a small metal disc at the bottom to keep the wick straight. This makes them about as mess-free as possible.

Tea-lights get their name because they were traditionally used in teapot warmers and in other contraptions designed to keep food hot, including fondue sets. There's a magic fondue spell later in the book...

Night-lights are similar to tea-lights. As I mentioned earlier, they were once commonly used to light bedrooms at night, but modern electric night-lights are considerably safer. Tea-lights typically burn for about 3 to 5 hours, although night-lights – as the name suggests – should burn all night long and usually have the duration marked on the casing.

Taper Candles and Dinner Candles

Designed to go into a standard candlestick or candelabra, these are so traditional they are almost certainly what springs to mind if someone mentions the word 'candle' – or 'fork handles', for those old enough to remember the Two Ronnies' comedy sketch. They are the kind you might put on the dinner table for a decoration that's a bit posher than a tea-light, which is why they are often called dinner candles, obviously. They are 'taper candles' because they are generally long and slim and taper to a bit of a point – a pleasing shape that's also practical. This is the shape created when candles are made by repeatedly dipping a wick in melted wax – the oldest method of manufacture. Taper candles are often used on Wiccan altars, usually in colours picked to represent the seasons. They can be used for spells too, of course.

Pillar Candles

Pillar candles are usually bigger and sturdier than taper candles and, let's face it, they are impressive. White church candles are a type of pillar candle and they do look superb in any ceremonial setting. If you have your own temple to do magic in, put a huge pillar candle on a tall stand and it not only sets the scene, but is also great to stand next to while doing a reading as part of a ritual. Pillar candles aren't always round and tall; they can be short and fat, square, triangular or fancy shapes. Some are huge and have multiple wicks. Pillar candles are usually referred to by their diameter and height when they are sold.

Container Candles

These get their name because they burn in the container they are made in. Like tea-lights they are relatively mess free, but are usually larger than tea-lights and last longer. The containers they come in can be lovely, especially those sold to be given as gifts. Once the original wax has gone you can reuse the container – either by popping a tea-light into it or making a new candle yourself. These are easy candles to make at home and great for combining spellcraft and candle making – more on that later.

Particularly relevant for spells or rituals are seven-day candles. As the name suggests, these are made to burn for seven days. There are two main types of seven-day candles. The first – the kind you are most likely to find in the UK – are often called memorial candles. They are designed to be left on the graves of departed loved-ones from one week to the next, between visits. Often for outdoor use, some will have a spike you can stick into the ground.

Other seven-day candles are specifically for spellwork or to petition the help of a deity or saint. These are more common in the US than in the UK, but you can find them for sale on the internet without much difficulty. They usually have a design on the container that either depicts a figure – a goddess, god, angel or saint for example – or symbols relevant to a specific spell, such as a four-leaf clover for luck. They can be used as pre-prepared spells; just light and leave. You can also add other components to them, such as scented oils.

Votive Candles

These are, by definition, intended for spiritual or religious devotions. One dictionary defines the word 'votive' as: 'An object offered in fulfilment of a vow, such as a candle used as a vigil light.' Some of the container candles I've mentioned above are essentially votives, but in the UK the term votive candle often means a free-standing candle, not in a container. They can be small, short candles, but are often marked by how long they will burn. They are perfect for offerings in temples or churches or for use while meditating or conducting a vigil.

Floating Candles

I love floating candles. These are usually round and smooth or flower-shaped, but can come in other designs such as butterflies or hearts. They look beautiful alight in a bowl of water and are especially used as wedding decorations, but I think they can be great for candle magic as well.

Spell Candles

Those big container candles I mentioned earlier can be called spell candles, but what I'm actually talking about here are small candles specifically designed for quick candle spells. They are like miniature dinner candles – usually about 1cm wide and 5cm or 6cm long. They can be bought in a huge range of colours so you can pick one that suits the spell. (There's a lot more on colour correspondences coming up next.) The reason these miniature candles are so great for candle spells is that they burn down fast. Some will last half an hour or so, some less. You need a suitably sized candleholder to put them in while you burn them, of course.

Some spell candles are mass-produced, but if you shop around you can buy handmade ones – and many witches prefer to use handcrafted items for their magic. Later on in this book I'll show you an extremely easy way to make your own spell candles – I do believe that anything you have made yourself will be most effective when it comes to doing magic.

Back in Victorian times candles of this size were used on Yule trees before electric fairy lights were invented, and they still are in some places. Obviously this poses a massive fire risk and shouldn't be attempted unless you watch the tree like a hawk and have a big fire extinguisher to hand.

Figures and Fancy Shapes

Candles can be moulded to look like pretty much anything. Around Yule you get snowmen and Santas, but you can also get them shaped like fruit, animals, people – even gods and goddesses. These can be used for spellwork or put on an altar as a representation of a deity or seasonal symbol, but think carefully about how well it fits in with what you intend before you use anything like this. You can use them to symbolise things wished for or powers you want to draw upon. Pagan supply shops sell figure candles of the type frequently used for magic. Two figures entwined are often used for love spells, cat shapes can be burnt for luck or protection and devils can be burnt for a bit of naughtiness if you are into that kind of thing (but do read the section on ethics first).

Another fancy shape sold specifically for spellwork is called the seven-knob candle. And before you start singing a song about a witch's candle having a knob on the end, this is actually formed from seven balls of wax on top of each other. You burn one ball each day for your spell to take effect. You can carve notches down the side of any old candle to divide it into seven sections if it doesn't have knobs to start with.

Tapers

Tapers are different to taper candles although the name sounds the same. These are long, wax-coated wicks used to take a flame from one candle to light others. They are useful when you are doing spells and rituals that involve lighting lots of candles because they are less fiddly than matches and also easier than lighting a candle with another ordinary candle. Personally, I rarely use them. I have a thing that looks like a wand and works like a gas lighter. You can also use a spill or even a stick of dried spaghetti to light candles. Sounds odd, but it works.

Cake Candles

As I mentioned earlier, making a wish over a birthday cake and blowing out all the candles is usually the first kind of candle magic anyone does. These little candles are great for candle spells too as they burn down really fast. I think you are never too old for this kind of magic – and it doesn't even have to be your birthday. Here is a cake candle spell you can do any time.

Cake and Candle Wishing Spell
All you need is a birthday cake candle and holder, and a cake. It can be any kind of cake you like; one you made yourself or one bought from a shop. I like a chocolate cupcake with lots of sprinkles.

Push the candle holder into the top of the cake and put the candle in it. Visualise your wish, light the candle and spend a few moments concentrating on what you want. Before the candle burns down completely, blow the candle out and imagine your wish being sent out to the universe. Remove the holder and remains of the candle and eat your cake – with a cup of tea or a glass of wine as you desire. Trust that the universe will hear your wish and respond...

Colour and Correspondences

Although it's always okay to use a plain white candle when working magic, colours make spells more effective. The reason is that colours have symbolic associations that witches call 'correspondences'. The more correspondences you add to any spell you cast the more powerful it is – and it is easy to buy coloured candles these days.

It is well known that colours can influence our moods and affect our emotions. Warm colours are cheerful, vibrant colours are exciting and cold colours are calming. There are also traditional cultural associations we grow up learning. Nowadays in the western world, pink is stereotypically used for a girl and blue for a boy, but before the 20th century it was the other way around – boys were dressed in pink because it was a subtle shade of manly red, while little girls were dressed in delicate shades of blue. White is associated with weddings in the west, but in parts of Asia white is the colour for funerals and red is considered better for bridal decorations.

Because colour associations vary from person to person, when picking a colour for a spell go with whatever feels right to you – that will work best. However, when you are stuck for an idea or want to learn what other witches have done, it can be useful to see the common correspondences attributed to various colours. I'm going to start with the four colours most often used by witches to represent the elements: yellow, red, blue and green.

Elemental Colours

Yellow
Yellow represents the sun, creativity, confidence, joy and happiness. It is the colour of ripe grain, sunflowers and honey. Natural beeswax candles are yellowish – although they vary in

shade from pale cream to dark amber. Use yellow for spells to cheer someone up, sweeten the mood, celebrate success or boost a creative project, particularly writing or communication. I often use yellow candles for money spells, because to me it is the colour of the abundance of the harvest and close to gold. In the past, yellow had less pleasant connotations – such as cowardice. In the *fin de siècle* of the Victorian era, yellow was the colour of decadence associated with Bohemian artists.

When casting a magical circle, some witches put a yellow candle in the east to represent the element of air, although in other traditions, including Tibetan Buddhism, yellow represents the element of earth.

Red

Red – the colour of fire, passion, sexual potency and desire – is best if you are after some fiery love in your life, but can also be used for anything you are passionate about. Burning a red candle can help you marshal your energies to champion a cause and fight for what you believe in. It can add more get-up-and-go to your life – so use it for spells to boost your willpower. Red is also the colour of blood and for that reason is associated with life-force, with the blood of a woman's monthly cycle and with the inside of the womb, fertility and motherhood.

When casting a magical circle, witches will often put a red candle in the south to represent the element of fire.

Blue

Blue is the colour of the sky and the sea, but also represents the spiritual and the sacred. Blue is worn by the Goddess Isis and the Virgin Mary. Hindu deities Krishna and Vishnu have blue bodies while Tibetan Buddhists use blue in art to represent transcendent wisdom. Light blue can symbolise a clear, daytime sky, while dark blue is the firmament at night. In spells, burn blue candles for peace, harmony, health, truth, honesty, wisdom, psychic and spiritual work, or during a Blue Moon. It can be used in magic to help you get a good night's sleep and for anything related to dreams, including lucid dreaming. Blue is a great colour to use for clear communication, as well as yellow. If you are facing a difficult conversation, burn a blue candle to help with clarity and mutual understanding.

When casting a magical circle, witches sometimes put a dark blue candle in the west to represent the element of water or a light blue one in the east to represent air.

Green
Nature is probably what springs to mind when you mention the colour green. Dark green is the colour of evergreens in winter while light green is new springtime shoots. It also represents environmental issues. Green candles are perfect for spells to help heal the planet, for fertility and regeneration, but the colour has far more correspondences in magic than just leaves, grass, growing things and recycling. In fact, after white, green is possibly the best colour to use for pretty much any spell. Green is associated with healing – the interiors of many hospitals are painted green because of the belief that this decor provides a good environment for people to get well. If you are doing a spell for healing, you can't go wrong using a green candle. Green repre-sents money too and you will frequently see it listed as the right colour for wealth spells – although I think this has something to with the fact that American dollars are green. Living in the UK where pounds sterling are gold-coloured coins, I use yellow or gold candles for money spells. Green can be used for love magic. I know that might seem odd, but historically light green was associated with growing love, romance and matters of the heart. The heart chakra (or centre of power in the body) is also visualised as green. Green candles can also be burnt in spells for good luck.

When casting a magical circle, witches often put a green candle in the north to represent living plants and the element of earth or one that is sea-green in the west to represent the element of water.

Black and White

Although black and white are, technically, absence of colour or all combined, in terms of candle magic they are very important because they represent opposites – day and night, summer and winter, hidden and revealed, for example. A pair of black and white candles can be used to represent polarity and also balance, such as the conscious and the subconscious, passive and active, male and female, yin and yang. Witches sometimes put both a black and a white candle on their altars at the equinoxes, when day and night are equal. You can use a pair of black and white candles for spells about bringing balance into your life or when two forces that might seem opposite are both needed to resolve a situation.

At other times you might want to use a black or white candle on their own for their specific correspondences.

White

While white is the default option and can be used instead of coloured candles, there are times when you choose to use a white candle because of its correspondences. White is associated with purity and peace. While all candles by their nature represent the power of light in a spiritual sense, a white candle does so more than any other. Use white candles for purification, protection, insight and to attract something into your life.

When casting a magical circle, some witches will put a white candle in the east to represent the element of air, because air is perceived to be colourless.

Black

Some people will refuse to use black candles because they associate them with evil. If that is the way you feel, fair enough, avoid black. Use a white candle instead – or maybe a dark blue or dark purple candle. However, I don't think any colour is inherently evil and most witches will occasionally feel a black candle is appropriate for some magical workings. Black candles are used to banish things from your life that are holding you back, such as bad habits or addictions. Black is also associated with mourning, death and the spirit world as well as protection. They can sometimes be used for purification. Light a black candle to honour a departed ancestor or loved one, or as part of a spell to communicate with their spirit. Halloween – or Samhain – is the time of year when witches are most likely to cast spells for those reasons. Luckily, it is also the time of year when black candles are easy to buy in high street shops. At other times of year black candles are hard to find except through specialist suppliers. My advice is stock up with a few at Halloween when you see them.

Some witches will put a black candle in the north of a magical circle to represent the element of earth.

Chakras, Rainbows and Multi-Colour Dream Candles

A famous list of colours is those of the rainbow – red, orange, yellow, green, blue, indigo and violet – colours that make up white light. These are similar to those attributed to the chakras – or energy centres associated with different parts of the body. These are useful correspondences for choosing colours in candle magic, so here is a list of chakra colour associations:

Red: Root chakra at the base of spine, relating to basic material needs
Orange: Sacral chakra in the lower abdomen, relating to physical desires
Yellow: Solar plexus chakra below the chest, relating to power and control
Green: Heart chakra in the middle of the chest, relating to love
Blue: Throat chakra, relating to communication

Indigo: Brow chakra in centre of forehead, relating to psychic senses

Violet: Crown chakra at the top of the head, related to spiritual connections

Having read that list you may feel you want a candle that will give you all of those things – and why not? You could get yourself a very pretty rainbow-striped candle or you could just burn a white candle because white light is all the colours of the rainbow combined; rainbows are created by refracted white light.

Pagan stores do sell multi-coloured candles for spellwork. You can buy double-action candles, which have one colour at the top and a second colour at the bottom. Triple-action candles have – you guessed it – three stripes. These are intended for when you want a double or triple dose of colour symbolism – say pink for romance first, then red for passion; or green for luck and purple to represent a legal matter. You get the idea.

Another type of two-colour candle is where you have a core of one colour and an outer layer of a second. Actually, many candles sold in regular high street shops that look coloured will be white on the inside with a thin veneer of red or green or gold or whatever outside. This is just so the manufacturer can save money on dye, but if you think it will do the job, use it.

Pagan supply shops sell candles with colours other than white on the inside. Ones that are red coated in black are sometimes called reversing candles and are intended to reverse bad luck or to send a curse back to where it came from.

Moving back to happier subjects, if you fancy a rainbow candle to wish for that proverbial pot of gold – they are available.

Colour Correspondences at a Glance
Here is an at-a-glance list of colours and their associations, including a few I haven't mentioned earlier:

Red: Passion, sex, love, courage, fire, basic material needs

Pink: Romantic love, friendship, emotional wellbeing

Orange: Energy, encouragement, physical desires, recovery after a set-back or break-up

Yellow: Cheerfulness, creativity, communication, happiness, the Sun, wealth, fruitful harvest, power, control

Brown/ochre: Earth, animals

Green: Nature, environmental issues, the Earth, health, wealth, love, luck

Blue: Communication, spirituality, peace, harmony, dreams, sea and sky

Indigo: Intuition, psychic abilities

Purple: Social status, legal matters

Violet: Wisdom, spirituality

Grey: Neutrality, balance, mists

Black: Purification, protection, hidden things, mourning and honouring the dead

White: Can be used for any spell because white contains all colours, but specifically associated with purity, peace, protection, the Moon

Gold: Prosperity and solar magic

Silver: Prosperity and lunar magic

Colour Tips

If you want to quickly add a bit of colour to a white candle, it can be rolled or dribbled in melted wax crayon. Another tip for marking candles is to buy a set of candle decorating pens. They are really easy to use and a set usually contains several different colours. You can write or draw straight onto the candle with them or you can inscribe a word or symbol and then infill it with colour, or make a stencil and tape it to the candle to help define your shape before colouring.

Exercise

Collect an assortment of coloured candles. Rummage around your home and gather up all the candles you already own. I'm a big fan of making the most of what I have rather than unnecessarily buying new stuff, it saves money and cuts down clutter. If you don't have many candles – or only have white ones – pop out and buy a few more in a variety of colours. They don't have to be expensive and it is easy to find candles in high street stores. However, if you can afford it, support specialist Pagan suppliers if possible.

At home, without lighting any of the candles, spend a little time meditating with the different colours. Make a note of the associations each has for you personally.

Afterwards, look at the list of correspondences given earlier and compare it with your own list. Remember, there is no right or wrong answer – trust your instincts.

Scent and Essential Oils

After colour, scent is the ingredient most frequently added to candles and is another way to give spells a boost.

You can buy a huge range of lusciously scented candles really just intended to make the room smell nice. They might be named after flowers, fruit or spices or have evocative names like 'Christmas Eve' or 'Home Sweet Home'. Although they might smell gorgeous, ordinary scented candles are frequently made using artificial perfumes rather than pure essential oils. In my opinion, artificial perfumes are not as good as natural ingredients when it comes to magic.

If you buy a ready-scented candle, check the ingredients. I recommend going to a specialist Pagan supplier or buying candles directly from someone who makes them so you can ask how they were made and what's gone into them.

Magical Correspondences
Essential oils – and other scents – have magical correspondences in a similar way to colours. Although I recommend using real essential oils rather than artificial perfumes to get the right correspondence for your spell, you can use dried herbs, spices and flowers if you prefer or if you don't have the right essential oil available. However, essential oils are easier to use in candle magic than dried herbs and have a more controllable level of scent. Always dilute a drop or two of any pure essential oil in a gentle carrier oil first. Pure essential oils are very flammable on their own as well as being harsh if you get any on your skin undiluted. You can put one or two drops of diluted scent directly on the top of a candle, poke a small hole or three into the wax and dribble oil in, or dress your candle with a scented anointing oil (more on this later).

As with colours, I recommend using what smells appropriate

to you personally rather than sticking rigidly to tables of correspondences someone else has drawn up. Mix and match to get the most from your magic.

Here is a useful list of scents to consider, but adapt this to suit yourself:

Almond: Almond oil is a common carrier oil. Magically it represents wealth and wisdom

Amber: Balance, ancestors, magic

Anise: Balance, energy

Bergamot: Friendship, happiness, combating depression

Catnip: Luck, love and, err, cats

Camphor: Disenchantment

Cedar: Balance, grounding

Chamomile: Health and healing, calmness, balance

Cinnamon: Both relaxing and stimulating, aphrodisiac, helps concentration

Citronella: Control, warding off bugs

Clary Sage: Purification, reducing stress, healing, boosting strength and aiding dream magic

Cloves: Abundance, tackling gossip

Copal: Purification, clarity

Cypress: Dealing with anger and grief, coping with change

Fennel: Courage, energy

Frankincense: Abundance, consecration, spirit, gods and goddesses

Gardenia: Dealing with fear

Geranium: Harmony, friendship, calmness, positive energy, overcoming addictions

Grapefruit: Energy

Heliotrope: Abundance

Hyssop: Grief

Jasmine: Balance, confidence, dreams, sensuality, relaxation, protection

Lavender: Balance, clarity, forgiveness, healing
Lemon: Stimulating, cleansing
Mastic: Abundance
Mint: Disenchantment
Myrrh: Abundance, consecration
Neroli: Courage, creativity, overcoming depression
Olive: Great carrier oil, abundance, wisdom, fertility, purity, victory, peace
Orange Blossom: Abundance, happiness
Patchouli: Creativity, grounding, sensuality
Pepper: Abundance, heat, also for some warding spells
Peppermint: Dreams, calming, cooling
Pine: Disenchantment, cleansing
Rose: Love and romance, happiness, contentment
Rosemary: Healing, love, protection, purification
Sandalwood: Psychic abilities, success
Vanilla: Love, sensuality, peace, dreams, luck, success
White Sage: Purification and cleansing, warding against negative energy, blessing, healing, calming
Vetivert: Grounding, earthiness, calming
Ylang ylang: Confidence, sensuality, passion, romance

Other Reasons for Using Scented Candles

Our sense of smell is primal and although humans aren't as good at detecting odours as some other animals, it is still one of the vital ways we get information about our environment. Scent evokes psychological and physiological responses and affects our mood. It not only helps us decide if things are nice or nasty, it also subconsciously sets the scene for us. Think of what comes to mind when you smell a sea breeze, baking bread, coffee or the pine smell of a Yule tree. This all means that, quite apart from magical correspondences, there are excellent reasons for using scented candles for spells and rituals.

Pleasure

You can light a scented candle just because you like the smell. There's nothing wrong with wanting to create a lovely atmosphere for a ritual or when doing spellwork. Simple acts of pleasure can in themselves honour the Goddess, as many witches will tell you.

Practicality

There are plenty of practical reasons to use certain scents – or avoid them. Citronella candles will keep bugs at bay – very practical when you are doing an outdoors ritual on a summer evening. The smell of peppermint is said to deter ants while camphor is used in moth balls. Don't go burning catnip outdoors unless you are casting a summon stray cat spell.

Mood Creation

As I mentioned earlier, smells create all sorts of moods. Just a hint of frankincense can make an ordinary room seem like a temple. You can buy scented candles with names that suggest an ambience, but do sniff them before buying as you might have quite a different reaction than the one implied. The same goes for applying essential oils to a candle yourself. Give the mix a good sniff first. For example, patchouli oil is meant to be sensual and good for creating a romantic atmosphere, but I know quite a few people who immediately think of hippie music festivals when they smell patchouli. If that isn't the mood you want, don't use it.

Aromatherapy

This complementary therapy uses essential oils to promote psychological and/or physical wellbeing. There is a big crossover between the aromatherapy uses for essential oils and their magical associations. Although aromatherapy can be combined with candle magic, they are slightly different. I don't have room to go into aromatherapy in detail in this book, but here are a few simple examples of aromatherapy effects you might want to combine with candle magic:

Relaxing and stress reduction: Lavender, chamomile, marjoram, orange, sage, ylang ylang, bergamot, geranium
Energising and uplifting: Lemon, orange, grapefruit, bergamot
Sensual: Ylang ylang, patchouli, lavender, rose, geranium, benzoin
Stimulating and aiding concentration: Peppermint, clary sage, rosemary

Always use genuine essential oils rather than artificial perfumes for aromatherapy.

Votive Offerings
Perfume is offered to gods and goddesses in many spiritual paths – and that is another way of using scented candles. Traditionally, incense is used for offerings of this kind, but there can be good reasons to use scented candles instead. Scented candles – or plain candles with essential oils – are safer and easier to use than incense. They are also easier to buy and often cheaper too. Choose an essential oil that is appropriate for the deity you are offering to.

Meditation
Filling the room with a familiar smell before meditation – or, indeed, before any ritual – helps create the right atmosphere and gives a sense of continuity. Long-lasting scented container candles can be ideal. They are reasonably safe and non-drippy so you can just light them, put them somewhere they aren't going to ignite anything and settle down to meditate while the aroma fills the space. Pick a candle that is appropriate for the type of meditation you want to do. I have a wonderful container candle

called Ebony Moon that I bought on a shopping trip in Glastonbury. It is black and is scented with amber, vetivert and clove. I light this when I am doing meditations during the dark phase of the Moon – a time for introspection and magic to gain insight into the root cause of problems.

Exercise
Go on another rummage around your home and gather any scented candles and/or essential oils you already own. If you haven't got many, pop out and buy a few bottles of essential oil. If you want a suggestion of what to start with, I recommend any out of lavender, orange, geranium, rosemary, sage and sandalwood, but feel free to pick others that take your fancy.

At home spend a little time meditating with each oil or scented candle and make a note of the associations each has for you. Afterwards, compare your own list with the lists of correspondences. As with colours, there is no right or wrong choice when it comes to magic – go with what feels right to you.

Herbs and Crystals, Bells and Whistles

While colour and scent are the main ways to boost candle spells, there are oodles of other things you can also use to make your magic work better. You can incorporate pretty much anything that symbolises your intention or represents the things or people your spell is about.

Spicing Things Up

Herbs and spices are really traditional spell ingredients. Witches add them to powders, potions and pouches as well as putting them into food for extra oomph and extra flavour. Dried flowers have similar uses. You can combine them all with candle magic for added correspondence power on top of colour and scent. Just sprinkle a pinch of finely ground herbs, spices or dried petals onto a candle before it is lit. Naturally, it won't stay there unless the candle is well melted, so you need to make sure the candle is in a suitably large and fireproof container to catch potentially burning bits of plant matter. Less messily, you can place the herbs and so on around the base of the candle and leave them there until the spell is complete, then sweep them up. Alternatively, put them into a jar or bottle and pop the candle on top of the lid or into the neck respectively.

Later in this book I discuss anointing or dressing candles with oil. If you do that, you can roll the sticky candle in herbs. Sprinkle them onto some greaseproof paper or into a dish larger than the size of the candle. Pick up your oily candle and roll it in the herbs until it is coated. Pop it into a holder and *voilà*, your candle is prepared. Do be aware that the herbs and oil won't be particularly well stuck in place and will come off on everything they contact. There is also a risk of them catching fire while the candle is burning down, so make sure the whole lot is in a suitable fireproof container – a big, cast iron cauldron is ideal.

Personally, when I use herbs in a candle spell, I like to bond them more permanently and less messily. If you make candles, you can add herbs to the melted wax, before pouring it into the mould or container, but not everyone has the time, patience or skill to do that. Here is a nice, easy trick to spice up your candles.

You need:
A candle
A deep container, big enough to put the candle in and that won't melt if it gets hot
Dried herbs associated with your magical intention
Hairdryer

You need the herbs to be quite fine. If they are too big and chunky, crush them with a pestle and mortar and then put them into the deep container. Use hot air from your hairdryer to slightly melt the candle's surface. Make sure you point the hairdryer away from the pot of dried herbs or you will blow them all over the place.

Roll the candle in the container of herbs so they stick to the candle. It's best to do this a little at a time. Just use the hairdryer on a few centimetres of candle and coat that bit with herbs, then move on to the next section of the candle and so on.

Every so often, leave the candle to cool and solidify, otherwise it will become too soft to handle.

Once the candle is coated in herbs, go over it with hot air a few more times so the wax really soaks into the herbs. You can do this several times, cooling it off in between. This both ensures the herbs have really stuck to the surface and the wax permeates through the herbs.

It might seem strange, but anything really soaked with wax is less likely to burst into flames, so there is less risk of accidents.

Another option is to slightly melt the wax on the sides of a candle by dipping the candle quickly into a pot of hot water. If you make your own candles, dip the candle into a pot of melted wax, then into herbs, then into the melted wax again.

Thyme Candle for Peace, Love and Courage
One of my favourite herbs to use in the way suggested above is thyme. Most people have dried thyme in the kitchen. It not only looks attractive as a candle coating, it also makes a wonderful magical candle that you could give as a gift to someone who is feeling poorly or having a tough time. According to *A Kitchen Witch's World of Magical Herbs and Plants*, by Rachel Patterson:

> [Thyme] is an excellent herb to use in any healing workings (and in culinary use for healing too). Also use it in incense blends to purify and cleanse your home and bring love and peace in. Thyme will increase your willpower and give you courage.

I think we could all do with those things from time to time. In order to enchant the candle while you coat it, visualise the person you are gifting it to receiving all of its benefits.

Here is a short list of some other common herbs and spices and their magical correspondences:

Basil: Protection, purification, love, astral projection
Cinnamon: Luck, love, passion, focus, concentration, energy, spirituality
Ginger: Warming, health, happiness, love, success
Mint: Clarity, money, healing, exorcism, protection, cleansing, calming
Parsley: Protection, happiness, cleansing, contacting spirits
Rosemary: Protection, cleansing, remembrance
Sage: Cleansing, purification and protection

Crystals

Crystals, gems and other stones have been used for magic since, well, the Stone Age. Their use for all kinds of spiritual and therapeutic purposes stills seems as popular as ever. You can combine crystals with candle magic by placing crystals around the base of the candle, popping a candle on top of a jar of crystals or even sticking very small ones to the wax – but do check that any stones you intend to use will be safe if they get hot. The magical use of crystals is a huge topic that I don't have space to cover in depth. One book on the subject worth reading is *Magic Crystals, Sacred Stones* by Mélusine Draco. Crystals can be added for their colour correspondences as there is often a magical correlation, but here is a brief list of a few common crystals and their symbolism:

Amber: Associated with wisdom, witchcraft and ancestral knowledge. Amber is solidified resin rather than a mineral. It is flammable, so don't let it come into contact with fire unless you mean to burn it

Amethyst: Spirituality, overcoming addictions, keeping a clear head

Black Tourmaline: Protection

Bloodstone: General purpose healing crystal

Citrine: Abundance, money, luck

Clear Quartz: One of the best general purpose crystals to add oomph to magic including health, luck and psychic development

Fluorite: Mental clarity

Jet: Purification, protection, healing grief, spiritual advancement, witchcraft. Jet is ancient wood that has mineralised under pressure

Malachite: Willpower, resolve

Obsidian: Grounding, protection

Onyx: Self-control, decision-making, luck

Rose Quartz: Love, romance, friendship

Smoky Quartz: Protection, grounding

Paper and Photos

The best way to dedicate a candle to a specific person or object is to use a small photograph. If you don't have a photo, you can write their name or draw a picture onto a slip of paper. I think words and symbols are best carved directly onto the candle, but it is quicker and less fiddly to put pen to paper, particularly if you want to write a missive or draw a complicated picture. You can place the candle on top of the paper or in front of it. (I'd say the latter is best if, for example, it is the only photo you have of your dearly departed granny who you need to contact to ask where she hid your inheritance.)

You can pin or stick paper to candles. It will attach well if you soak the paper thoroughly in melted wax and then stick it in place before it sets. The wax will also help make it less flammable, although any paper that comes into contact with a flame will burn. I know this should be obvious, but I'm saying it anyway; put the candle and paper into a suitable fire-proof container first. Yes, witches really do have lots of uses for nice, flame-proof metal cauldrons.

Bells and Whistles

When I need to cast a spell I often look through various books of magic first to get ideas. However, I usually find I don't have all the things that are supposed to be necessary. I think it is only in novels and movies that witches have shelves and cupboards stuffed with every magical ingredient possible. In order to find the things you want – or substitutes for things you want but don't have – it's time for a scavenger hunt, which I think is the fun part. Spellwork should be fun!

You really can use all sorts of odds and ends to add correspondences, symbolism, personalisation and connections to spells. If you want to find a suitable marriage partner, you could put the wedding ring of a beloved ancestor in front of the candle. You could boost a spell for a safe journey with the little boat or car figure from a Monopoly set – or use one of the plastic houses if you are looking for your dream home. Do be careful not to melt the plastic – it smells foul, is toxic and your dream home may burn down...

I use whatever I can find that might have the right correspondence to substitute for missing components. Perhaps a spell calls for dragon's blood resin to boost courage, offer protection and increase magical potency, but I don't have any. Looking around I see I do have a tenacious weed in my garden called alkanet and the roots were once used for their rich red dye. Maybe that would do as a substitute? Alternatively, I have a cuddly toy dragon. Maybe a tiny clipping of red plushy fur would be fine? You get the idea. Be inventive.

As for real bells and whistles – yes, you can get candle bell chimes. The heat from tea-lights in the bottom spins a disc at the top decorated with angels, fairies or birds that strike small bells as they go round. Traditionally, the sound of bells attracts good spirits and banishes harmful influences. My aunt had one that she used to light on Christmas Eve. I used to find it lovely at first, but after a while it really got on my nerves – wonder what that says about me?

Candlesticks, Tea-Light Holders, Bottles and Jars

Unless you only buy container candles, you need holders. This is, of course, mainly to stop candles falling over and making a mess or setting fire to your carpet, but it is nice to have holders that look the part and add to the magical effect.

I have a pair of antique brass candlesticks I use on my altar, another antique holder with a handle and a deep dish that is good for carrying around indoors, a small candlestick for spell candles, a large holder with a pointy spike in the middle for wide candles and several tea-light holders in various colours. I also have candle lanterns for outdoor use.

You can add colour correspondences to your spells by popping white candles in coloured glass containers. Even choosing a candlestick of a suitable colour can boost your intent. You can mould your own holders out of clay and paint symbols on them once the clay has hardened. Firm fruit such as apples can be cored and a candle inserted in the hole (perfect in spells for bounty, health, love or fairy magic). Halloween pumpkin lanterns can also be turned to spell use – more on that in seasonal magic.

If the candles don't quite fit the holders, you can get things similar to pencil sharpeners that whittle down the ends of candles to resize them. A bit of dripped wax can also be used to keep a candle upright, but do make sure the candle is secure.

Witch Bottles

Another type of traditional spell is the witch bottle. In bygone centuries in England these were really just used as protection magic and they didn't have anything to do with candles. The idea was you put a few pins inside a bottle then filled it up with pee (yes, spells were icky back then) and corked it. Then you buried the bottle under your front doorstep to block any curses sent your way. Nowadays, bottle spells are used for a whole range of purposes (and they don't normally involve bodily fluids). So, what's that got to do with candle magic? Well, the modern type of bottle spell can be magically charged with a candle. You put all the things that correspond to your spell's purpose inside the bottle – apart from the candle. You pop in photos, tiny slips of paper or long letters, herbs, flowers, crystals, coins, Monopoly pieces or whatever else might add symbolism. Stick a candle in the neck, light it while speaking your intent, then let it burn almost completely down leaving the waxy stub to seal the spell. Keep the bottle somewhere safe – on your altar, on a shelf, under your bed or, if you are traditional, buried under your doorstep.

To recharge the spell and give it an extra boost, relight the old stub and when it is a bit melted stick a fresh candle on top. This is more difficult to do if it is buried in your garden...

In hoodoo folk magic, jars are more often used for this kind of magic than bottles. I seem to end up with more empty bottles than jars for some reason, but if you are the other way around then by all means use a jar. The neck of a jar is larger so it is easier to pop bigger items inside. You can bang a small nail in the lid of the jar (pointy bit upwards) to affix your candle.

Purification and Anointing

Earlier I wrote about using essential oils for their magical properties of scent, but oils can also be used to purify and cleanse candles. This doesn't mean cleaning physical dirt off them, it means clearing off past associations, influences or negative energy. Mind you, if they are a bit grubby, a bit of cleansing will do both jobs.

The reason you ritually purify candles is that those made in big factories, which have sat around on supermarket shelves and been passed from person to person, can pick up all sorts of energy and associations along the way that won't be conducive to your spell working the way you want. If you have made the candles yourself with a magical purpose in mind or they have been specially prepared by a Pagan supplier for spellwork, then cleansing could actually be counterproductive.

Cleansing
Put a small amount of virgin olive oil into a dish about the size of an egg cup. Put a small amount of salt into another dish. Place a hand over the olive oil and visualise white light cleansing it. Say: 'May this oil be blessed, purified and consecrated.'

Then put your hand over the salt and say: 'May this salt be blessed and consecrated.'

Add a tiny pinch of salt to the oil and stir it in clockwise or sunwise (what witches call *deosil*). You can use your finger to do this or, if you want to be really witchy, use the tip of a knife called an athame. The athame is the second type of knife a witch often has (the boline I mentioned earlier being the first). It is used for actual magical stuff, including blessing oil, water, wine or whatever.

Take a clean cloth (or a piece of kitchen towel), dip it in the oil and salt mix, and wipe the candle with it from top to bottom. Say:

'May this candle be cleansed and purified.'

One thing I should also mention is that salt has the effect of making a candle drip less and burn longer. However, salt can affect the scent of essential oils, so bear that in mind.

Here are some other ways of cleansing and purifying your candles:

- Leave them in your window in sunlight all day on a Saturday, which is associated with cleansing, but don't do this on a very hot day as no one wants a droopy candle.
- Leave them in a window under moonlight on the night of a Full Moon.
- Pass them through the smoke of a burning smudge stick, which is a bundle of dried herbs such as white sage.
- Sprinkle them with droplets of salty water. If you do this, avoid the wick because, obviously, wet wicks don't burn well.

Anointing or Dressing

If you feel your candles are pure enough anyway, you might still like to anoint or 'dress' them – something pretty much always done using oil. It is a way of preparing your candle for the work that lies ahead, dedicating it for its purpose and putting extra magical energy into it.

You can simply anoint your candle with a plain oil such as olive or almond (avoid almond oil if you are allergic to nuts). As mentioned earlier, this can also be used as a carrier for appropriate essential oils to add correspondences. Pour a little carrier oil into a small dish and add a drop or two of the scent or scents that symbolise the right message for your spell or ritual.

Most standard books on candle magic say that the way to anoint or dress a candle is to rub the oil all over it, starting from the middle and working up to the top, then from the middle to the bottom. I've found this works fine, although an alternative is to start from the top and work downwards if you are doing banishing spells and start from the bottom and work upwards if you are doing a spell for attraction or accumulation. Some people prefer to do that in reverse, with the idea that applying oil downwards is drawing it in and applying oil from the bottom to the top is sending it out into the universe. Do what feels right to you for the spell you are doing.

There are a few other methods. Pick whichever appeals depending on how messy you like to get. (As much as I might like to sometimes see other people covered in oil, I don't particularly enjoy having sticky paws myself – and please avoid using any oils you are likely to react badly to.)

- Pour oil onto the palms of your hands and rub the candle between them until it is all oiled up.
- Dip the tip of a finger or two into the oil and apply to the candle with gentle strokes (is this beginning to sound a bit suggestive?)
- Using a small brush, paint the oil onto the candle.
- Drizzle oil onto the candle using a dropper. This won't cover it as evenly as the other methods, but that doesn't matter.

If you are using container candles or tea-lights, you might not be able to get them out of their jars or cases to anoint the sides. That's fine; just anoint the top of the candle, rubbing the oil deosil (sunwise) around the wick.

While you are anointing the candle, you may visualise the intended purpose of any spell or ritual you have planned and, if you like, state your intent too.

When to Cast Your Spell

If you need to cast a spell quickly, the best time to do it is now. Don't let anyone else tell you otherwise. Your urgency and desire will help make it work. If you put the spell off until the weekend or until the Moon is full, or whatever, the magic of the moment could have dissipated.

However, when magic isn't urgent, it is best to find out when the time is right – the ideal phase of the Moon and day of the week.

Phases of the Moon

Most witches will tell you magic works best under a Full Moon – and I agree. That's one of the reasons most covens meet when the Moon is full. The other reason is that it is really hard to see what you're doing at night out on blasted heaths (or the modern equivalent) unless there's plenty of moonlight.

I'm not suggesting you should only do candle spells and rituals outdoors. In fact, unless you have pretty good windproof lanterns, it is much better to do candle magic indoors. But the cycles of the Moon are a hugely powerful force when it comes to witchcraft.

I'm going to briefly explain the phases of the Moon because although most people are well aware that the Moon has a 28-day cycle, it isn't always taught in schools and I've had to explain it to a few novice witches in the past. Every month, the Moon wanes from being a full, round, silvery disc in the sky to being kind of oval-shaped (gibbous), then a half disc, then a crescent, which thins and thins until the time of the Dark Moon, when you can't see it in the sky at all for about three nights running. Then you start to see a tiny crescent again – the New Moon. That crescent waxes back to a half Moon, which fattens until it is full again.

For some reason, magic seems to work best when the Moon is

full. Maybe that is connected to the fact that the tides are highest then, or that people act a bit crazier under a Full Moon – I don't know. Magic isn't science, it is more like in Star Wars when Luke is told: 'Feel the Force around you.' Witches just feel the force of magic most strongly under a Full Moon. That's about as far as I'm going into magical theory for the moment.

So, if you want to cast a spell, find out what phase the Moon is in. You can usually do that by checking in your diary or just Googling it.

The time of the New Moon is considered good for any spell that is about new beginnings, for example if you want help with a project you are starting or a change of job or new love in your life. The waxing Moon – that means the phase from the New Moon to the Full Moon, when the Moon is getting bigger – are great when you cast spells for things to increase – maybe money or opportunities coming your way. The waning Moon, which is decreasing in size, is perfect if you want help losing weight or are trying to give up smoking or could do with your workload being lessened. Half Moons are suitable for spells about getting things in balance – perhaps to get people to discuss things evenly after a row or to gain a sense of calm in your life. The time of the Dark Moon is best for divination, to get insight into things that are bothering you, to uncover the truth in matters and to work out how to proceed in the future.

Days of the Week

In my experience, while witches look to the Moon, magicians seem to pay more attention to the power of the days of the week. But, the more things that line up to make a spell work, the better. Below are some of the magical correspondences for each day.

Monday
Planet: Moon
Colours: Silver, white, blue

Deities: Diana, Artemis, Selene, Luna
Correspondences: Women's mysteries, illusion, glamour, sleep, peace, beauty, prophecy, dreams, emotions, travel, fertility, insight, wisdom

Tuesday
Planet: Mars
Colours: Red, black, orange
Deities: Mars, Ares, Tiwaz
Correspondences: Battles, courage, victory, success, strength, conviction, rebellion, defence, wards, protection, anything military

Wednesday
Planet: Mercury
Colours: Purple, orange
Deities: Mercury, Hermes, Woden
Correspondences: Communication, the arts, writing, transport, change, luck, gambling, fortune, chance, creativity, making deals, solving crimes, work issues needing discussion

Thursday
Planet: Jupiter
Colours: Blue, purple, green
Deities: Thor, Jupiter, Juno
Correspondences: Abundance, protection, prosperity, strength, wealth, healing, management roles

Friday
Planet: Venus
Colours: Pink, aqua/green
Deities: Venus, Aphrodite, Freya
Correspondences: Love, birth, fertility, romance, gentleness, pregnancy, friendship, passion, happiness.

Saturday
Planet: Saturn
Colours: Black, purple
Deities: Saturn, Hecate
Correspondences: Banishing, protection, wisdom, spirituality, cleansing, astral magic, weeding the garden or gathering crops, honouring or remembering the dead

Sunday
Planet: Sun
Colours: Gold, yellow
Deities: Brigit, Helios, Apollo
Correspondences: Success, fame, wealth, prosperity, promotion, getting a new job

I Am Lovely Spell

Yes, you are lovely, as is everyone, but sometimes we all need to be reminded and here is a spell to help you using the power of the Moon and day of the week as well as other candle magic lore from earlier in the book.

This spell is most potent on a Friday at or near a Full Moon. You need a pink or sea-green candle, or a white tea-light in a pink or sea-green glass holder. On the side of the candle, carve the words: 'I am lovely.' Anoint the candle with a little olive oil into which you have put a drop or two of rose or rosemary essential oil. Light the candle and say: 'Aphrodite, Goddess of Love and Beauty, please grant me your blessings.'

While the candle is lit, spend some time pampering yourself. Run a bath and pour your favourite bath oils into it, give yourself a beauty treatment, put on your favourite clothes that make you feel wonderful and eat your favourite food. Have the candle with you at all times to add its magic to your pamper session.

Moving it all About

Let's get our candles moving about. Get an image in your mind of the sorcerer's apprentice from Disney's Fantasia waving a wand to get mops marching around with buckets of water and doing the housework. Now let's move on to more realistic things. (But it would be great to be able to do that kind of magic, wouldn't it?)

What I'm actually going to describe is a type of candle spell that takes a bit more time, space and effort than the ones I've covered up to now. You will need a permanent or semi-permanent altar, a reasonable amount of time, a lot of candles and a big metal tray to put the candles on for safety reasons.

Because of the complexity, some people call these types of spells 'candle rituals', but I still classify them primarily as spells. The basic idea is that you pick two, three or even more candles to represent the people, things or situations you want to affect. You cleanse, carve and anoint them, put them on the tray on your altar and light them, say words representing what you want to happen, then gradually move the candles closer to each other, or further away from each other, or round each other, depending on your intention. You repeat the procedure over several nights, weeks or even months.

For example, if you are trying to make up with a friend after an argument, attract a lover, bring in more money or get a new job, you would pick one candle to represent yourself, one to represent the other factor, and bring them closer together. To rid yourself of an addiction, encourage mice to move out of your kitchen, or cool your relationship with someone, move the candles further away from each other. To be kept at the centre of a situation, you might circle several candles around the one that represents yourself.

As I mention next, in ethics, if you are doing a spell that might affect another person, get their permission first or add the words: 'An' it harm none.' Harming anyone with magic is just as mean as harming them any other way. (Oh and if you really want the mice to move out of your kitchen, get a cat. All witches need a cat anyway.)

Let's start with the altar.

You might already have an altar – a place where you do magic or honour the deities or your ancestors – but if you don't then it is very easy to set one up. It can be a coffee table, the top of a chest of drawers, bedside cabinet or sturdy wooden box. It doesn't have to be a permanent fixture, but you will need to leave it set up for at least a week. Ideally it should be in a position where you, your children or your pets are not going to knock everything off it.

On the altar, you will need to put everything required to cast the spell – don't forget the metal tray to place the candles on for safety, a box of matches or lighter and a candle snuffer. You can also put seasonal flowers, a statue of a goddess or god, incense, shells, feathers or anything else that feels magical to you.

Now the candles: you will need candles with long enough durations to last until the very end of the spell. They should also be stable enough that they won't easily fall or be knocked over. You can select colours and scents in the way described earlier for suitable correspondences. If you pick candles with very strong scent then you probably won't need to burn incense as well, but if you have unscented candles, pick an incense blend that matches your intention.

This is how the basic moving candle ritual works:

- Turn off any electric lights and other electrical devices in your room (mobile phone/TV/computer or whatever).
- Light the altar candle and any incense.
- Take three deep breaths in and out and clear your mind to focus on the spellwork.

- Place the candles representing the spell's focus in their starting positions on the altar.
- Light the candles while concentrating on your intention.
- Say any words, such as: 'By the power of these candles, may my wishes be granted. May X happen, an' it harm none. By the power of these candles, so mote it be.'
- You can say these words three times for added effect.
- Move the lit candles a centimetre or so in the desired direction.
- Spend a few moments longer in front of your altar visualising your desired effect.
- Snuff out all of the candles.
- Leave the candles exactly where they are on your altar until the next day, then repeat the ritual, moving the candles a little bit more in the intended direction. When the candles nearly touch each other – or reach the edge of the altar – let them burn down completely.
- After that, the stubs and candle holders can be removed from the altar and everything tidied up.

This seems a good place to comment on the best way to extinguish candles. Magically, it is one of those hotly debated subjects – should you blow, pinch or snuff? Well, I would say always snuff candles out unless your spell specifically requires something else (such as birthday cake wishing). The reason for this is safety. You could burn yourself if you pinch a lighted wick, while blowing can send sparks flying. If you don't have a snuffer, use a metal spoon.

I've included a few moving candle spells in this book, but if this type of candle magic appeals, then a classic text on the subject is *Practical Candle Burning: Spells and Rituals for Every Purpose* by Raymond Buckland. This was written back in the heady occult days of the early 1970s and has been reprinted and updated several times since. Most of it is a grimoire of spells following the format above, with suitable words to say for all manner of magical intentions. One thing that is unusual about the book is that every spell has two versions – one Christian and one Pagan. They are pretty identical in terms of the candles used, but the Christian versions have words from the Bible – usually psalms – while the Pagan versions have other poetry or call on Pagan gods and goddesses.

I think this demonstrates that you don't have to be Pagan to cast spells. Although most modern witches are Pagan, in the past few centuries many witches would have been Christian and called on the saints or recited psalms. I have frequently asked the help of St Anthony, patron saint of lost things, when something has gone missing – although I have also called upon Fortuna, Goddess of Luck, to help me find what I am looking for. Address your words to whatever you believe in – gods, goddesses, ancestors, angels, saints, spirits of nature or just faith in the power of the human mind – your strength of belief is what counts most.

Ethics and Curses

The question of ethics is hotly debated by modern witches. Many believe it is wrong to cast any spell on a specific person without their permission, including love spells and even healing spells.

My own view is a little less cut-and-dried. I think it is polite to ask someone if they want you to send them healing wishes before you do so, but if they are unconscious after a car accident then do what you feel is best to help them recover. On the question of love, I am all in favour of there being more romance in the world. If you are single and fancy a chance of getting together with someone who is also single, what is the harm in that?

What I would say is that you should always think very carefully about the consequences of your actions – and that includes spells. Even a simple spell for wealth could leave you feeling very guilty if an inheritance came to you because someone died. It is a good idea to always add the words: 'An' it harm none.' That's the traditional witchy get-out clause.

Many witches also say you should never cast curses, even against someone who has done you a terrible injustice. While I agree it is wrong to use magic to try to physically harm anyone, I do think there can sometimes be a place in the modern world for magic that uses a little sting in order to right wrongs.

At Bath, in England, many curse tablets were found at the sacred springs of Sulis Minerva, Goddess of Wisdom and a champion of just causes. The curses were written on tiny strips of metal and then thrown into the hot pools. Quite a few were from people who had been stolen from and who wanted their items returned and the thief punished.

In modern times if something has been stolen I always recommend first going to the police and checking insurance policies. If you want to do magic to help get your things back, start with gentle spells (there are some in the next chapter). If that doesn't work, I can't see that there is anything terribly unethical about the following slightly more grey spell, loosely based on the ancient traditions in Bath.

Spell to Curse a Thief

You need a bowl of water, a floating candle, two altar candles, a small strip of paper, a pen and a pinch of a hot spice – use whatever you have in the kitchen such as black pepper, paprika, ginger or chilli powder. You will also need space to set up an altar, something to represent the Goddess Sulis Minerva (this could be a goddess candle or statue or a picture of the famous golden head of Sulis Minerva from Bath), some incense and a glass of pure spring water. Oh and don't forget a box of matches or a lighter.

Set up a small altar. Light the altar candles on either side of the Sulis Minerva image and light the incense too. In front of these, place all the other items. Put a pinch of hot spice into the bowl of water. Light the floating candle.

Write the following on the slip of paper: 'Sulis Minerva, Wise Goddess, please help me in my request. May the person who has my (insert details of whatever was stolen) feel the hot stings of guilt on their conscience until it is returned to me.'

Read the words aloud, then roll up the paper and light it with the flame of the floating candle. Hold it over the bowl of water. Before the flames reach your fingers and burn you, drop the ashes and remaining charred paper into the bowl of water.

Sit in front of the altar while the floating candle burns and give thanks to Sulis Minerva while sipping the glass of pure spring water. When there is just a small amount of spring water left in the glass, pour that into the water in the candle bowl as a libation to Sulis Minerva.

Ideally, let the floating candle burn down completely. When it goes out, remove it from the bowl and take the water outside to pour onto the ground with the ashes, spices and burnt paper scraps.

Wax Poppets, Talismans and Amulets

There's a reason this bit comes after ethics, and that's because poppets are similar to what are commonly called 'voodoo dolls'. They are dolls made to represent a person and then enchanted so that, by sympathetic magic, whatever you do to the doll has an effect on the person. Sticking pins in the doll with the intention of causing pain to the person represented is a nasty thing to do and would generally be considered black magic. However, you can also use poppets for healing magic – wrap a bandage round the doll or give it a drop of medicine – or to communicate with someone by talking to the doll if you can't do that by normal means. You can even create a poppet to represent yourself and then really pamper it to make yourself feel good.

The reason I am mentioning poppets in a book about candle magic is that one way of making a poppet is to form it from melted candle wax.

To do this, get a metal gingerbread figure cookie cutter. Put it on some greaseproof paper then drip wax inside until it is a good thickness. Leave it to set hard before carefully removing it. You then visualise the doll as the person you want to represent and name it by saying three times: 'I name you (X).'

Small things connected to the person in question can be added to the wax to link it to them more closely. Strands of hair or fingernail clippings are traditional, if a bit gross. You could use a thread from something they have worn.

Amulets and talismans can also be created from candle wax. An amulet is an object that has intrinsic power to give protection to its wearer, whereas a talisman is specifically made to achieve a particular purpose. Amulets give protection by absorbing negative energies, while talismans work by generating a positive force to achieve their objective.

To make either from wax, form it into a suitable shape and

then carve words or symbols onto the surface. Keep it on your altar or in a suitable place for its effect to be felt. For example, you might make a house-shaped wax amulet to protect your home or a star-shaped wax talisman to get success in a project. As with the poppets, state three times what you want the talisman or amulet to do and visualise the end result.

Grimoire

A grimoire is a collection of spells. There are quite a few spells dotted around this book and given as examples and exercises for specific techniques. Here are some more candle spells for various purposes.

Daytime Wishing Spell

You need:
White or yellow tea-light candle
A sunny day

Although you can cast the spell at any time of the year when the sun is shining, I think it is a perfect summertime spell. Stand facing a window through which sunlight is shining, or where you can see the sun in the sky. Strike the match and hold it in one hand, while holding the unlit tea-light candle in the other and look out of the window (never stare directly at the sun, however, as that can seriously harm your eyes). Think clearly of what you wish for, then say:

All I ask on this sunny day
Is send the wish I want my way.

Light the candle, put it in a tea-light holder and let it burn right down. Personally, I like to place it near me while I get on with work or chores, so that I can glance at it from time to time.

Night-Time Wishing Spell

You need:
A white, silver or dark blue tea-light candle

Light a candle in the evening, make a wish and say:

Candle light
Candle bright
Grant me this
My wish tonight

Ideally, let the candle burn right down.

A Spell for Springtime Wishes

Here is a lovely but simple spell that is perfect to cast in early spring – although you can do it at any time of year. It will help your wishes and dreams come true. You can work the magic alone, with your partner, with a group of friends or as part of a springtime ritual.

You need:
A floating candle for each person
Glass bowl or cauldron of water

Everyone taking part should scratch their wish on the bottom of a candle, light it and float it on the water. When all the candles are lit, dance around the bowl or cauldron and chant three times:

Fire and water
Kindle and flow
Bring life to our dreams
And let them grow.

Enjoy watching the candles burn down, perhaps while enjoying some good food and drink.

Big Hugs Candle Magic

Here's a little spell to give you a magical warm hug when you are feeling down, either physically or emotionally.

You need:
Tea-light
Jar or glass candle holder
Paper
Sticky tape

You could pick a pink candle to help you feel 'in the pink', but you can use a white tea-light if you prefer. Find a clear glass jar or candle holder giving plenty of room around the tea-light, then measure a wide strip of paper long enough to wrap around the jar. Cut a chain of paper dolls from the strip.

The way you do this is to fold the paper into pleats and then, with the paper folded, draw half a doll shape on the top fold, with half a head and body against one edge of the paper and the hands and feet touching against the other edge. Cut out the shapes through all the layers of paper and unfold to reveal your row of dolls holding hands. If you like, you can draw or paint features and clothes on the dolls or you can leave them plain. Tape the dolls around the outside of the jar or candle holder.

Take the tea-light out of its container for a moment and rub the candle between your hands a few times, then put it back into the metal container before popping it into the jar. If you want to scent the candle, give it a little spray of your favourite perfume or essential oil before lighting it.

Light the candle and visualise yourself feeling hugged and loved.

Have the candle burning somewhere near to you and let the candle burn down completely if possible – but don't leave it unattended.

You can reuse your chain of hugging dolls and jar as often as you like. Pop a new candle in when you feel you want a magical hug.

Wax Heart Love Talisman

Earlier I explained that a talisman is a magical item made to achieve a particular purpose, usually created by the person who wants magical help. Here is how to make a love talisman when you want to draw romance and passion into your life.

You need:
Red or pink taper or dinner candle
Dried rose petals
Heart-shaped metal cookie cutter
Greaseproof paper
Heatproof tray

This spell should ideally be done on a Friday, which is associated with Aphrodite, Goddess of love.

Place the cookie cutter on some greaseproof paper on the heatproof tray.

Sprinkle a few rose petals inside the cookie cutter. As you do so, say:

Goddess Aphrodite, as I sprinkle these rose petals, I ask you to charge them with the power to attract love to me.

Light the candle and say:

Goddess Aphrodite, as I light this candle, I ask you to charge it with the power to attract love to me.

Then, drip the wax from the candle slowly into the cookie cutter, covering the rose petals and building up a heart-shaped layer of wax that is at least 1cm thick. While you are doing this say:

Goddess Aphrodite, as I create this talisman of the heart, I ask you to charge it with the power to attract love to me.

When you have finished, leave the wax heart to cool. Once it is solid, pop the wax heart out of the cookie cutter, peel off the greaseproof paper and your talisman is ready. Keep it somewhere that you associate with love and passion – ideally the bedroom.

I would add that once you have what you want and the talisman has done its job, give thanks to Aphrodite then break the talisman, releasing its powers to attract love back into the universe. If you don't, you might end up with more lovers than you can handle.

Magic Fondue Spell

This is the perfect spell to stir up some fun with fellow witches, just slightly inspired by Shakespeare's Macbeth (sometimes referred to as The Scottish Play for reasons connected with witchcraft – if you are curious, look it up in Wikipedia).

You need:
Fondue set with a ceramic bowl heated by a candle
Tea-light
Cocktail sticks for marking the candle
400g dark chocolate
85g unsalted butter
284ml double cream
300ml milk
Marshmallows and/or strawberries
Small wooden spoon
Fondue forks

Everyone present takes it in turn to carve their initials into the tea-light before it is popped under the ceramic bowl. Then put the chocolate, butter, cream and milk into the bowl and light the candle below it. While the ingredients are melting, everyone takes it in turns to stir the fondue with the spoon, secretly making a wish then saying out loud:

Double, double toil and trouble,
Chocolate melt and fondue bubble.
Candle burn and grant my wish,
Serve me up a delightful dish.

When the fondue is ready, dip the strawberries and marsh-mallows into it and enjoy.

Message in a Bottle

This is a spell for when you want to get a message across but can't do so for real. There could be all sorts of reasons for that – perhaps you want to say things to a lover who has left you or a dearly departed relative, perhaps you don't know how well your message will be received or quite who to address it to. You are sending the message out like the castaway of fiction putting a message into a bottle and throwing it into the ocean, trusting someone will find it, read and respond. These days chucking a bottle into the sea or any waterway would be unacceptable littering, so this spell is a great alternative.

Write your message by hand, ideally onto handmade writing paper, but any nice notepaper will do. Write as much as you like; you can really bare your soul and say all you want. Roll the letter up, tie a ribbon round it, and slide it inside a bottle. Put a dinner candle into the bottle's neck like a candleholder. You might need to trim the bottom of the candle first to make it fit. Light the candle and imagine your message being cast into the ocean of the universe. You don't have to burn this candle all in one go and you can reuse your bottle candleholder as often as you like. When you feel your letter has been received and answered, recycle the bottle and paper responsibly.

Preserved Memories

Here's a keepsake spell to remember a special moment. It's intended for occasions such as holidays, birthdays, weddings, anniversaries and the like where you might have a nice bottle of wine, tin of sweets or even a special jar of breakfast marmalade and also get cards or other mementos. If you are on holiday you can use postcards or photos, tickets for events you enjoyed, leaflets about things you saw or whatever. If the original is too precious to damage, take a colour photocopy. Use decoupage techniques to stick the images to the outside of the bottle, tin or jar.

On a piece of paper write the date, occasion, your name and the names of those with you as well as jotting down a list of all the things you want to remember. Roll the paper up and pop it inside the container. You can also put other small things inside – shells or small stones from the beach for example. Put a candle in a bottle neck or fix a candle on to the top of a jar or tin. Holding the bottle or jar, think about all the happy memories you want to preserve. Focus your thoughts and feelings into the bottle. You could say something like:

Spirits of the land, sea and sky; spirits of this place; I thank you for this wonderful time and ask your blessings. Let me keep this to remind me in the months to come of this time and place and those who are with me.

Light the candle. You don't have to burn it all the way down, relight it when you feel like doing so to remember the happy times. When it is nearly all melted you may stick a fresh candle on top of the old stub.

Circle of Protection
Later in this book I describe using a candle to cast a ritual circle, but a candle can be used to cast a quick circle of protection around yourself against negative energy or an unpleasant atmosphere. Just light a candle and place it near you. Visualise the light from the candle spreading all around you. Say or visualise the words:

May the light of this candle protect me, keeping out all baneful influences.

Obviously no candle is going to keep out physical dangers and you shouldn't light a candle anywhere it is unsafe to have a naked flame.

May There be Peace in This House

This is a good spell to cast in a building that is fraught with arguments, disagreements and bad feelings. It is very simple.

Take a white candle and anoint it with pure olive oil. Put it in a candle holder designed to be carried around safely – a lantern, for example. Light it and say:

May there be peace in this house.

Carry the lantern through the entire building, walking around each room carefully, saying:

May there be peace in this room.

When you have finished, put the candle somewhere safe and ideally let it burn down completely – though you should never leave lit candles unattended, even in lanterns. If you have to go out before the candle is completely burnt, relight it and continue burning it at the next opportunity.

Spell for Get Well Wishes

This spell is great to cheer up someone who is unwell, and speed their way to recovery.

You need:

A green or white candle

A lovely bunch of flowers or a potted plant such as chrysanthemums, which symbolise cheerfulness

Place the candle in front of the flowers and light it. Staring into the candle flame, with the flowers behind it, think about the person who needs healing. Try to picture them in your mind and then visualise sending them a beam of healing energy from the candle flame, through the flowers.

You could try visualising the energy as a ray of green light, because green is often considered to be a healing colour. If saying some words will help you focus your intention, simply repeat the phrase:

Get well soon.

Continue this for as long as feels appropriate.

When you visit the person who is ill, give them the flowers as a present to cheer them up even more.

Recovering Lost or Stolen Items

You need:
White candle to represent yourself
Black or other dark candle to represent the thing you have lost
Olive oil
Permanent or semi-permanent altar

Carve your name on the white candle and carve the name of the missing item on the dark candle. Anoint both candles with olive oil. Place them on your altar, at least 18cm apart. Light both candles and say the following words while concentrating on being reunited with your item.

May that which was lost be found,
May that which was taken be returned,
May that which is hidden be revealed,
May that which was mine be mine again.

Then, move the candles a centimetre towards each other (2cm in total). Snuff the candles out. Do this for nine nights or until you get your item back. When the candles are nearly touching, let them burn right down.

Spell for money

You need:
Large jar with a wide metal lid
Yellow or gold tea-light candles
A shiny coin
A citrine (known as the stone of prosperity)

First cast the spell on a Sunday when the Moon is waxing or full. Before you begin, cleanse all the items. Wash the jar, coin and citrine in salty water and wipe the candle with olive oil. Hold up the jar and say:

I charge this jar to store
My saved wealth
And bring me more.

Then, place the pound coin and citrine into the jar and say:

Bring me silver
Bring me gold
Bring me riches
Manifold

Then put the lid on the jar, put the tea-light on top of the lid and light it. Repeat the spell every week, putting a further cleansed coin into the jar, repeating the words and lighting a tea-light. Do not take any of the coins out until you have got the money you wanted or a year and a day has passed. Then take the money out and buy yourself a treat.

To Get a Job

You need:
Orange candle to represent yourself
Yellow candle to represent your ideal job
Almond or olive oil
Sandalwood essential oil
A permanent or semi-permanent altar (or other suitable space)

Ideally, cast this spell on a Wednesday or a Sunday. Carve your name on the first candle and carve either the word 'job' or the title of the job you want on the second candle. Put a few drops of sandalwood essential oil into the almond or olive oil and anoint both candles with this. Place them on your altar, at least 20cm apart. Light both candles and visualise being given the job you want. Then, move the candles 1cm towards each other. Snuff the candles out. Repeat this every Wednesday or Sunday or until you get a job. When the candles are nearly touching, let them burn right down. You do also need to apply for jobs as well as casting the spell.

Spell to Cut Ties

Use this if you want to move on from a situation, but feel your links to it are holding you back. This could be after a relationship break-up, the end of a job, moving home or cutting links with people you feel are holding you back. Do bear in mind that you are not intending to harm anyone with this spell, just sever your own emotional or psychic links with them.

You need:
Black or white candle
Length of wool

Flameproof dish or cauldron

Light the candle. Hold the wool up in front of the flame and say:

This length of wool represents my links to (X), which I wish to sever.

Then hold the wool taut in the flame of the candle until it has burnt through. (Be careful not to burn yourself or set light to anything except the wool). Say:

As this wool is burnt in two, so my links to (X) are no more.

Drop the remaining bits of wool into the flameproof dish or cauldron. Extinguish the candle.

Two

Ceremonies and Rituals

Basics of Ritual

Up to now this book has mostly been about spells, which are individual acts of magic for a specific purpose. They are usually short and simple. Magic rituals tend to be longer and more complicated, and can be a framework in which spells are cast. In witchcraft, casting the circle is the main formalised ritual or part of a longer one.

Rituals are ceremonies in which the words and actions follow a prescribed form. They can follow cultural, spiritual or religious traditions – such as seasonal celebrations and rites of worship. Modern Pagan witches will often honour deities associated with the seasonal festivals as part of their rituals.

Candles are often an important part of these rites – including in the casting of the circle itself.

This section covers using candles for devotional purposes, casting a circle and the use of candles within seasonal ceremonies as well as more spells you can do as part of a ritual.

Altars and Altar Candles

I've mentioned altars a few times already in this book, as places to do magic, but I'm going to go into more detail here. Okay, let's get down to basics, why do witches have altars? On a purely practical level, as well as being somewhere to do spells, they are a good place to put the bits and bobs – the ritual tools – needed for magical or ritual work. This includes the witches' knives (the athame and boline), incense, wand and any spell ingredients, but often the first thing put on the altar is a ceremonial candle. This illuminates the work to be done, other candles are lit from it and it symbolises the spark of energy the ritual starts and ends with. The first act of a ritual is often to light the altar candle and the last act is to extinguish it.

There may well be other things on your altar too, such as food and drink, seasonal flowers and small statues or pictures of deities you honour. Make sure your altar is sturdy and stable and that the holders for your ceremonial candles keep them securely upright. You don't want your ritual prematurely ended with a candle falling over and setting light to your altar cloth or the curtains.

Pure white candles can be used at any time, but many witches like to represent the seasons with suitably coloured candles. There's more on that under seasonal celebrations.

As well as candles, don't forget to put on your altar something to light the first candle with, tapers (or a stick of dry spaghetti) to light further candles, and a snuffer to extinguish flames.

Even if you are just casting a single candle spell rather than performing a full ritual, an altar is a good place to do it. An altar can also be a place where you light a candle while meditating or as an act of devotion to a god, goddess or ancestor. It can be a permanent fixture if you have space, or a small table you set up as and when required. I have a good sized wooden box that I keep candles and other ritual items inside, the top of which can be used as my altar in the home or outside.

Circle Casting

Most modern Pagan witches cast a circle before doing spellwork, conducting ceremonies or celebrating the seasonal festivals of the year. A circle is a sacred space.

But why a circle? Well, there are many reasons given, but among them are the fact that a circle has no beginning and no end, it symbolises strength, unity, the cycles of life and eternity. It is an ideal shape for raising magical energy inside and keeping unwanted influences outside. It also looks neat.

If you have done any witchcraft, you have probably already cast a circle or two, but here I'm going to explore some ways of circle casting with an emphasis on the role of candles. You can use these ideas or stick to any other methods you are familiar with.

Before I go into more detail, here is an at-a-glance list of the circle-casting process:

1) Preparation: set up the things you need for the ritual.
2) Purification: cleanse the sacred space, those taking part in the ritual and items you feel need cleansing.
3) Cast the circle.
4) Welcome the directions and their associated elements: east/air, south/fire, west/water, north/earth and sometimes above and below.
5) Raise magical energy.
6) Do the required magical or spiritual work, which can include spells, meditation, prayers or other devotions and seasonal celebrations.
7) Share cakes and wine (or bread and fruit juice if you prefer).
8) Say thanks and farewell to any deities honoured and to the directions.
9) Take down (or open) the circle.

Preparation

Let's get one thing straight – actually, let's get one thing round, as circles aren't straight, are they? You do not need to physically mark or represent a circle when you cast one, so you don't need chalk, string or a nice circular shag-pile rug unless you want one. You will need plenty of candles in suitable holders, matches or a lighter, anything you are going to use for your spells or devotions, a little food and drink to share and the altar to put your bits and pieces on. You can put the altar in the centre or at the northern edge of the space. You might like incense, but this is optional. Athames, bolines and wands are also optional unless your specific rite requires them.

More on Cleansing and Purification

Earlier I wrote about cleansing your candles, but you can also use candles to cleanse and purify the area for your circle. I'm not talking about using beeswax to bring a shine to the altar – although beeswax does make the best furniture polish. As with purifying the candles, you are clearing your space of unwanted energy and also clearing your mind of unwanted thoughts so you can fully focus on the task at hand. You don't want to bring your everyday cares and worries with you when you are going to do anything magical. It will detract from the focus you are putting into the spell.

Let's start at the beginning. Tidy up the room you are going to do your spell in at least a bit. You don't have to totally spring-clean, but put clutter away and vacuum the carpet. Okay, if you want to be totally traditional you should probably sweep up the dust with a besom broom, but we are living in the 21st century and vacuuming is a whole lot quicker. Save the besom for a quick ceremonial sweep after you've used the tech to do the hard work if you want to.

Then have a nice bath or shower and put on clean clothes. Some witches have a special robe just for being witchy in, but that isn't essential. In fact, wearing any clothes at all isn't essential, but if naturism isn't your thing I would recommend wearing something loose and comfortable. I have a lovely long black velvet dress I wear if I want to impress other witches; if I'm on my own I sometimes just wear my dressing gown – although that is long and black too. What I would say is that if you are doing spells that involve a lot of lit candles make sure you wear something that is reasonably safe from going up in flames. Droopy sleeves are not advisable.

Now, on to the magical cleansing.

Light a single candle on your altar then turn off all the other lights. Stand, sit or kneel before the candle. It will seem as though the glow grows brighter as your eyes become accustomed to the reduced illumination. Imagine you are bathing in the candlelight. Be still and breathe gently in and out at least three times. Allow your body and mind to calm right down.

Then, stare directly into the flame of the candle and whisper quietly, asking it to take away any thoughts on your mind that might distract you from your purpose. For example, you might say: 'Flame, take away my work stresses. Take away my thoughts about what I'm going to cook for dinner. Take away my annoyance over the row I had with my friend earlier.'

Spend as long as you need to, then a moment or two longer. When you are sure you have cleared your mind as much as you can, you can say:

Candle, candle burning bright,
Take away my doubts and fright
Transform my worries into light.
Clear my mind for this magic rite.

This purification is not designed to banish your problems completely. Asking the flame to transform your stress about work isn't going to make your work stress go away completely, but will help keep your mind off it for a while. You can do this at other times too – it doesn't just have to be before casting a circle.

Purifying Items
Candlelight can also be used to cleanse and purify items that you intend to use for magic – especially things that might be damaged if you wash them in water – sets of tarot cards, delicate flowers or soluble crystals, for example.

Just pass the item three times through the light of the candle after you have cleansed and purified yourself. If it is at all flammable then make sure it doesn't catch fire in the flame. On the third pass, say something like:

By the candlelight and the power of three, may this object be cleansed.

Some rituals – such as consecrations – ask that items are purified by each of the four elements: earth, air, water and fire. In that case, a candle flame is usually used for the element of fire. A shake of salt can represent earth, smoke from burning incense or a smudge stick can represent air and a light sprinkling of water is, err, water.

Casting the Circle
The circle is cast to contain any magical energy you raise and to keep out unwanted influences. Obviously, it isn't a physical barrier – it won't keep out your cat or your children – but it will help keep out negative psychic energy. Here is a way to cast a circle using a candle. Take an unlit candle and light it from the one you used for purification. Go to the northernmost edge of the space that is to be your circle, then walk around the circumference of the circle three times sunwise (deosil), visualising the light of the candle flame building up an invisible barrier that stretches up over your head and down under your feet in a globe

all around your space. The circle needs to be large enough for yourself and anyone with you to move about in. End up back in the north and then put the candle down on your altar. Do make sure you use a candleholder suitable for carrying a candle safely.

Directions and Elements

The next part of the ritual is to go around the circle again and welcome each direction and its associated element – east/air, south/fire, west/water and north/earth. These are sometimes called 'quarters' of the circle and it is customary to light a candle at each of these positions. Look back at the chapter on colours to pick appropriate ones to use.

When it comes to the elements, many witches use incense to represent air and a candle to represent fire. They will also use physical representations of earth and water. But you can use a candle for all four elements. Obviously, the flame represents fire. The solid wax body of the candle represents earth and the liquid, melted wax represents water. The smoke and shimmering air around the flame represent air.

Scented oil diffusers – the kind made of pottery with a tea-light in the base and a bowl for essential oil mixed with water above that – also represent the four elements. Pottery is made from clay and is earth, the lit candle is fire, the water is water, and the scented vapour that rises when the essential oils evaporate represents air.

So long as you pick your essential oils carefully, this can replace incense on your altar. A small candle and a little hot water are not only safer than burning charcoal, but evaporated essential oils are a lot easier on the lungs than solid incense. There is also less risk of setting off the smoke alarm and having burly firefighters rush in to save you. Of course, if you fancy being rescued by burly firefighters...

Raising Energy

Raising magical energy before you cast your spell really adds to its power and effectiveness. The most common ways of raising energy are chanting, singing, dancing or drumming. Do whatever feels right for you; just make sure you stay within your circle.

Do Your Magic, Honour Your Gods

Cast your spell, light your sacred flame, ask for the blessings of a god, goddess or beloved ancestor, read a poem or sing a song and light a candle of the appropriate colour to celebrate the season. As witches say: 'Do as you will, but harm none.'

Cakes and Wine

After the spells are cast, it is traditional to give thanks to any deities you may have called upon – or to the land, the sky and the universe in general – by raising a toast with a glass of wine or fruit juice and then doing the same with a piece of cake or bread. Leave a little wine and a few crumbs to put outside after the ritual as an offering to nature and the spirits of the place.

Farewells

Say thanks and farewell to the directions and the elements. This is usually done by going round the circle widdershins (anti-clockwise), stopping at each compass point and saying thanks and farewell at each and putting out the quarter candles.

Taking Down the Circle

At the very end of your ritual, you should take down the circle. This is often called 'opening' it. Walk around the edge in a widdershins (anticlockwise) direction and visualise the energy of the circle withdrawing. When you get back to the altar, blow out the candle you used to cast the circle with and say:

The circle is open.

Candle Ritual to Send Healing

Here is a full ritual suitable for a single person or a group and is a variation on the ritual format just outlined. In this, all the parts can be done by a single person, but for groups I've divided the words into four parts labelled Ritualist A, Ritualist B etc. It is best done at the time of the Full Moon.

You need:
Broom for sweeping
Cauldron
Lighter or matches
Candles: pair of white altar candles, white pillar candle, four candles for the quarters
Tapers or similar
Salt and water in small bowls
Anointing oil
Snuffer
Cakes or bread
Wine or fruit juice

Set-up
The altar is put in the north with small bowls of salt, water and olive oil mixed with a few drops of essential oil. At the start of the ritual, the only light should be any natural moonlight and a large pillar candle, alight in the centre of the ritual space inside a cauldron or other large fireproof container.

Sweeping and Purification
The area is swept with the broom, then all gather in the ritual space and sit around the cauldron or large dish with the lit candle in it.

Ritualist A: *'May the light of the candle bring peace. May it free us of doubts and worries. Let us meditate on the flame.'*

All: Meditate on the flame for a moment, then stand up in a circle.

Ritualist B: Goes to the altar and mixes the salt with the water. They then bring the salt and water mixture to the cauldron and pass the bowl through the light of the candle flame (being careful not to burn their fingers). They say: *'May this salt and water be blessed.'*

They then go around the circle sprinkling a little salt and water at the perimeter and say: *'May this circle and all within be purified with salt and water.'* They then replace the bowl on the altar.

Ritualist C: Goes to the altar, picks up one of the white altar candles and anoints it with the oil. They light this from the cauldron candle and say: *'May this oil and flame, symbols of air and fire, be blessed.'*

They then go around the circle with the scented candle and say: *'May this circle and all within be purified with air and fire.'*

Then they replace the lit candle on the altar.

Casting the Circle

Ritualist D: Picks up the second white altar candle and lights this from the cauldron candle too. They say: *'May the blessings of spirit fill this flame.'*

They then go around the circle with the blessed candle and say: *'May all within this circle be protected by the blessings and powers of spirit.'*

They replace the second lit candle on the altar.

Calling the Quarters/Elements:

The four unlit candles intended to represent the elements/directions of air/east, fire/south, water/west and earth/north are then picked up in turn. Each is lit from the cauldron candle and taken to the respective direction/quarter of the circle, while the following words are said:

Ritualist A (East): *'I call upon the east, the element of air, to be welcome in our circle.'*
All: *'Hail and Welcome!'*
Ritualist B (South): *'I call upon the south, the element of fire, to be welcome in our circle.'*
All: *'Hail and Welcome!'*
Ritualist C (West): *'I call upon the west, the element of water, to be welcome in our circle.'*
All: *'Hail and Welcome!'*
Ritualist D (North): *'I call upon the north, the element of earth, to be welcome in our circle.'*
All: *'Hail and Welcome!'*

Raising Energy

All: Hold hands and dance around the cauldron to raise energy. Singing or chanting can be done too. This continues until everyone feels energy has been raised or until everyone has danced enough.

Healing Magic

Ritualist A: Says: *'Now we send healing to those who need it.'*
All: Everyone in turn calls out the name of someone they are sending healing energy to, with a few words about what healing is needed and why. If this is being done with a single person in mind, then everyone calls the same name. However, healing magic can be sent to different individuals – no more than one person per ritualist. This kind of healing magic can also be done for animals, plants, areas of land or the planet in general.

Honouring the God/Goddess

All sit around the cauldron again. Everyone takes it in turn to call the name of a god or goddess they wish to honour.

Example 1: *'I call upon Candelifera, she who bears the candle. Goddess of childbirth, life and new beginnings, I ask you to grant us your blessings!'*
Example 2: *'I call upon Jupiter. God of abundance, prosperity and good health, I ask you to grant us your blessings!'*

Cakes and Wine

The cakes and wine (or bread and fruit juice) should be held so that the candlelight falls on them.

Ritualist B: *'May this food and drink be infused with the power of spirit and blessed by the God and Goddess.'*
All: *'Blessed Be!'*
Ritualist C: *'We thank the deities for their blessings.'*

Farewell to the Quarters

Ritualists who called the quarters say: *'Element of earth/ water/fire/air, we thank you for attending our rite and bid you hail and farewell!'* Each quarter candle is then snuffed out.

Opening the Circle

One person snuffs out the two altar candles.

Ritualist D: *'This circle is opened. May we go in peace and love.'*
All: *'May we meet again in peace and love.'*

Outdoor Candles

Candles look beautiful outdoors at night, especially on warm summer evenings. They can be incorporated in rituals and ceremonies out in nature; citronella candles and garden flares will have a double purpose of keeping bugs and insects at bay as well as providing a light source. Do bear in mind that safety is just as much an issue outdoors as indoors, as is tidiness. Be careful not to damage natural sites and take all your litter home with you, including cases for tea-lights.

Below are some ideas for outdoor candle ceremonies and rites.

Candlelit Procession

As a child I fell in love with the idea of candlelit processions when watching the Disney cartoon Fantasia. A reverent candlelit walk to a holy well, stone circle, hilltop mound, forest grove or other magical place is the perfect prelude to a night of witchery or a vigil to watch the sunrise at the Solstice dawn. But, you need to have a suitable candle lantern.

You need a lantern you can carry easily, that won't get too hot or set light to anything and will survive a strong wind. Ornate garden candle lanterns aren't necessarily designed to be carried. Make sure you buy one that is. Ideally, you want one where the handle doesn't get too warm to hold, the bottom is okay to set down on normal surfaces, and the sides don't get so hot they will burn you if you accidentally touch them. You want one where the flame isn't going to set fire to anything and where wax isn't going to drip out. Most of all, you want one that is going to stay lit.

I have found tea-lights tend to go out when they are moved around too much – this is because all the wax in the casing melts, so joggling it will slop the wax everywhere – either flooding the wick or spilling all over the inside of the lantern. It is better to find a lantern that holds a pillar candle.

Camping and outdoor suppliers sell hurricane lanterns for 9-hour pillar candles where the candle is securely held in place even when you walk around with it; the holder, base and sides stay reasonably cool and there is minimal risk of causing damage to yourself or the environment.

Sharing the Light: A Candle Ceremony

This is a lovely ceremony to do outdoors. There should be one central candle. This could be a large candle within a cauldron or it could be a garden flare. Everyone taking part in the ceremony needs their own candle, preferably in a wind-proof container. You also need a taper.

One person lights the central candle and everyone stands around it in a circle, holding their unlit candles.

The person who lit the candle says: *'Let us all share in the light of our circle, in friendship and love.'*

They then take the taper, light it from the central candle and light their own candle. They then pass the taper, still alight, to the person next to them and say: *'I share this light with you, in love and friendship.'*

The person taking the taper says: *'Blessed be.'*

They light their own candle and this continues until all the candles are lit.

Finally, the first person says: *'Blessed be the light of friendship and love.'*

All repeat this.

Static Outdoor Illumination

Candles are fabulous for static outdoor lighting. Here's where you can use all those pretty ornamental candle lanterns that aren't suitable for dancing about with. Or you can pop tea-lights in jam jars – that works as well and is very cheap.

If you want to make a handle for a jam jar, tie some wire firmly around the edge with a loop over the top – but do be aware that the opening and handle will get extremely hot once the candle is lit. If you want to hang up the jam jar, get a lantern stand with a hook that is made for the purpose.

As well as just having a selection of pretty garden lights dotted around, here are a few other ways of delineating space outdoors after dark using candle lanterns (the tea-lights in jam jars option is also perfect for when you need a really large quantity):

- Mark the route of a path using candles along either edge.
- Set candles around the circumference of a circle before casting it as a magical space. Put appropriately coloured glass candle holders at the four quarters (east, south, west and north) with plain lanterns or jars for the rest of the circle.
- Lay out tea-lights in a spiral or labyrinth for a walking meditation. Do make sure you leave enough space between the lights for people to safely walk without risk of setting light to the hems of their clothes.
- Set tea-lights out as star signs or other symbols. These work best if you can look down on them, so putting them on a lawn that can be seen from an upstairs window or from a raised terrace works well.

Candles for Seasonal Celebrations

Most modern Pagan witches celebrate eight seasonal festivals that they call the Wheel of the Year. They are: Imbolc or the first stirrings of spring; Spring Equinox when day and night are equal length; Beltane or May Day; the Summer Solstice; Lammas (sometimes called Lughnasadh) or start of the harvest; Autumn Equinox when day and night are equal once more; Samhain or Halloween; and Yule or the Midwinter Solstice. Candles of suitable colours for the season can be put on the altar along with seasonal flowers. Here are some suggested colours for the Wheel of the Year:

Imbolc: White
Spring Equinox: One dark and one light candle, often black and white
Beltane: Green
Summer Solstice: Yellow
Lammas: Orange
Autumn Equinox: One dark and one light candle, often black and white
Samhain: Black
Yule: Red, sometimes together with dark green

Four of these festivals – Imbolc, Beltane, Lammas and Samhain – are based on traditional Celtic fire festivals, when bonfires were lit. The celebrations could involve jumping over bonfires or running between two fires. One way of representing this using candles rather than real bonfires is to light candles and place them inside cauldrons or similar fireproof containers and jump over or between them instead. Although this is safer than a bonfire – and a good indoor option – you do still need to be careful not to ignite your clothing.

Spring

Imbolc/Candlemas

Pagans celebrate the first stirrings of spring at Imbolc, on February 1. Although snow may still be falling, snowdrops are just starting to bud as harbingers of new life. It is a festival sacred to Brigit, Goddess of healing, poetry, smithing and other crafts. She is associated with holy wells. Pagan rituals to honour Brigit often include lighting white candles, reciting poetry and visiting holy wells or sacred springs. If you choose to combine all three, please make sure your candle is in a lantern that will retain any wax drippings and not set fire to anything – and take any tea-light holders, candle stubs and other leftovers away with you afterwards so as not to leave litter.

In Christian traditions, the festival of Candlemas (or Candle Mass) falls on February 2 and is when a priest blesses beeswax candles for use in church during the year ahead. Some are also given to members of the congregation to use at home. You might have noticed I am not averse to borrowing Christian traditions from time to time and this is one I love to include in Pagan rituals at Imbolc (although it is possible that Candlemas itself was based on an earlier, ancient Pagan tradition). You can cleanse all your candles using the instructions given earlier in this book or you can have a go at making candles. Call upon the Goddess Brigit to give them her blessings.

In Poland, Candlemas is called *Święto Matki Bożej Gromnicznej* (the Feast of Our Lady of Thunder Candles). Candles blessed on this day are called *gromnice*. These are lit during thunder storms and placed in windows to protect the home from damage and ward off the worst of bad weather.

Earth Hour

This modern, world-wide event organised by the World Wide Fund for Nature encourages people to turn off non-essential lights for one hour from 8.30pm to 9.30pm on the last Saturday in March every year. Many Pagans conduct candle-lit ceremonies to heal the Earth at this time and you could adapt the Candle Ritual to Send Healing from earlier in this book.

Spring Equinox

On March 20 or 21 the day and night are of equal length and it is a time for balance. A suitable thing to do is to make changes on a personal level. After lighting two candles on your altar – one dark and one light – make two lists. One is of things you plan to put behind you, such as habits, behaviour patterns or relationships that are holding you back; the other is of things you want to grow within your life, such as things you want to learn or do, activities you want to try and new relationships you wish to cultivate.

Spring Equinox usually occurs close to Easter and can be celebrated in similar ways. Instead of giving chocolate eggs you could give egg-shaped candles as gifts. You could also light an egg-shaped candle while thinking about the things you want to hatch into your life. A deity often honoured at the time of the Spring Equinox is the Anglo-Saxon Goddess Eostre, associated with the spring and with hares and eggs.

May Eve and Beltane (May Day)

May Day or Beltane, on May 1, has been celebrated as a time for festivities for centuries, if not millennia. The evening before, or May Eve, is also considered a magical time – ideal for spells, witchery and divination, especially for matters of love and romance. It would be a very auspicious time to try candle divination.

According to Morgan Daimler in the book *Pagan Portals: Irish Paganism*, an Irish candle tradition is associated with May Day. She translates from *Sanas Cormaic B102*:

A widespread tradition was the placement of a 'May bush', a branch or bough of a tree (sometimes hawthorn or holly) that was placed by the front door for luck and decorated with yellow flowers, brightly colored ribbons, and egg shells (Danaher, 1972). On the night of May Day candles might be lit on or around the bush and people would gather and dance around it.

She also notes a ceremony from Laois, Ireland, which '...called for the head of the family to light a candle and bless the door, hearth, and the four corners of the home, as well as each family member from oldest to youngest, and then the area around the home where a rowan branch should be placed.'

Summer

Summer is the time for celebrating outdoors and candles are the perfect lighting for magical ceremonies whether in your own back garden or at a sacred site. Try out any of the outdoor candle suggestions given earlier.

Summer Solstice

The Summer Solstice, or the longest day, is on June 20 or 21 each year. Where I live, in London, the night is a little over 7 hours long from Solstice Eve to Solstice Dawn and could be watched with a candle vigil from sunset to sunrise.

In Ireland at Midsummer there is a longstanding tradition of honouring Aine, Fairy Queen and Goddess of summer, with a torch-lit procession on the hill of Knockainey, County Limerick, and other high places.

St John's Eve

On St John's Eve – the evening of June 23 – it was traditional to light bonfire beacons on hilltops and for people to jump over bonfires. As mentioned earlier, candles are safer to jump than bonfires and make an acceptable substitute where naked flames are not allowed.

Autumn

Autumn Equinox
The night and day are again of equal length between September 21 and 23. It is another time of balance. As for the Spring Equinox, burn dark and light candles and make two lists, one giving thanks for the harvest and what you have achieved in your own life, another listing the preparations to make for the winter to come, on a personal and practical level.

Halloween or Samhain
Pumpkin lanterns seem as much a part of Halloween as ghoulies and ghosties and things that go bump in the night, but when I was a kid pumpkins weren't easily available in England. We did make Halloween lanterns, but instead of hollowing out pumpkins, cutting a face in them and popping a candle inside, we carved them out of turnips and swedes. These are the most obstinate vegetables to carve. You have to hack at them with sharp implements, brute force and the determination of a horror-movie psycho-killer – even then the resulting lantern is best described as malformed. But malformed is probably good. The idea behind them is that by putting a monstrous face in your window you ward off supernatural nasties, because they would not wish to go near anything that looked uglier than themselves.

An old name is Jack o' lantern, supposedly after an Irish trickster called Stingy Jack who conned the Devil into paying for his drinks. The Devil, outraged at being fooled, refused to let Jack into Hell after he had died, leaving him to wander the Earth in darkness for eternity, with only a single coal to light his way. In parts of Somerset, Jack o' lanterns are called Punkies, and Punkie Night is celebrated on the last Thursday of October. Like

Halloween, on Punkie Night, children go from door to door in a tradition similar to Trick or Treat. They carry around Punkies made from hollowed mangel-wurzels – a large root vegetable often used as cattle feed – and demand gifts with the rhyme:

It's Punkie Night tonight
It's Punkie Night tonight
Adam and Eve would not believe
It's Punkie Night tonight
Give me a candle, give me light
If you haven't a candle, a penny's all right.
It's Punkie Night tonight.

Pagans tend to call October 31 Samhain rather than Halloween, and it is a time to honour the ancestors. It is believed that the veil between this world and the next is thin at this time of year. In modern witchcraft rituals, candles are lit and the beloved dead invited to join the living, then all the candles and any other lights are extinguished. Those present sit in darkness, waiting for messages from those who have passed over. The candles are then relit and scrying – or divination – by candlelight is performed.

In *Pagan Portals: Irish Paganism*, Morgan Daimler says that in former times in Ireland, Samhain was a three-day celebration:

It was an old practice in Ireland to light a candle for each deceased member of the family and to leave the doors unlocked – in some cases even open – and to leave out either fresh water or porridge as an offering to those ancestors who chose to visit.

Winter

The long dark nights are the time when candles really come to the fore. They give the home a warm glow quite apart from any ritual, celebratory or ceremonial uses. Many cultures have festivals at this time of year in which it is traditional to light candles including the Jewish festival Hanukkah, and Diwali, the Hindu festival of lights, as well as Christmas. Pagans celebrate Yule or the Winter Solstice on December 21, the longest night of the year.

Advent

While Christians might light an advent candle with 24 sections inscribed on it to burn each day from December 1 until Christmas Eve, Pagans can mark a candle with 21 sections to mark the countdown to the Winter Solstice.

St Lucy's (or Lucia's) Day

This is on December 13 and is another festival of light honoured in parts of Europe and Scandinavia. St Lucy is represented by a young woman wearing a white dress and red sash with a crown or wreath of candles on her head. There is evidence this festival may date back to pre-Christian times and that St Lucy was originally seen as a goddess.

Yule and the Midwinter Solstice

Wreaths and boughs of evergreens brought into the home for midwinter celebrations are ancient traditions – although the trees themselves and lights on them only became popular in Victorian times in England. Back then the lights were small candles. Obviously, electric fairy lights are much safer.

The Yule log is another popular tradition that might originate from Germanic Paganism and was associated with the burning of a large candle. In 1725, historian Henry Bourne wrote about a possible origin for this in Anglo-Saxon Paganism:

Our Fore-Fathers, when the common Devious of *Eve* were over, and Night was come on, were wont to light up *Candles* of an uncommon Size, which were called *Christmas-Candles*, and to lay a *Log* of Wood upon the Fire, which they termed a *Yule-Clog*, or *Christmas-Block*. These were to illuminate the House, aud [*sic*] turn the Night into Day; which custom, in some Measure, is still kept up in the Northern Parts. It hath, in all probability, been derived from the *Saxons*. For *Bede* tells us, That [*sic*] this very Night was observed in this Land before, by the *Heathen Saxons*. They began, says he, their Year on the Eight of the Calends of *January*, which is now our *Christmas-Day*: And the very Night before, which is now Holy to us, was by them called *Mædrenack*, or the *Night of the Mothers* ... The *Yule-Clog* therefore hath probably been a Part of those Ceremonies which were perform'd that Night's Ceremonies. It seems to have been used, as an Emblem of the return of the *Sun*, and the lengthening of the Days...

One modern Pagan witchcraft tradition is to place four candles on a log during Winter Solstice celebrations, light them and watch how they burn down. Each candle represents a season of the year to come and the way it burns and shapes left by dripping wax can be used to predict what might happen in the year ahead.

Devotional Candles,
Sacred and Eternal Flames

Sacred Flames

Many traditions from all over the world have, since ancient times, had flames that burn constantly and continuously. They are often called eternal flames and usually have great cultural, spiritual or religious significance. They can commemorate a person or historical event, be a reminder of dedication to a common goal, represent divine or mystical presence within a church or temple, or be kept alive as a sacred duty by flame-keepers in perpetual honour of a deity. One of the most famous was the sacred fire of the Goddess Vesta in Ancient Rome, which burned in her circular temple. Vestal Virgins were selected by lot and served for 30 years, tending the holy fire that represented the heart and health of the city. The rites of Vesta ended in 394CE by order of the Christian Emperor Theodosius I and the fire was extinguished.

In Irish mythology, the goddess Brigit was honoured with the burning of a sacred flame. In the Middle Ages, she was syncretised with a Christian saint of the same name, who was also associated with sacred flames, particularly one maintained by 19 nuns at her sanctuary in Kildare. This may earlier have been a shrine to the Goddess Brigit.

Other historic eternal flames include one in the Temple of Apollo at Delphi, in Greece, and also the Olympic Flame, which has been revived for the modern Olympic Games. There are other modern, public examples of eternal flames. Many countries have a Tomb of the Unknown Soldier, commemorating the dead of World War One, with a flame that burns continuously.

In historic times, eternal flames were often fuelled by wood or oil and while modern public perpetual flames usually employ piped gas, there are some inspiring examples of sacred flames represented by candles kept alight within the homes and temples of Pagans. One such sacred flame is at the Glastonbury Goddess Temple and is called the Flame of Avalon.

The Flame of Avalon

The Flame of Avalon was first lit on the last day of the 2004 Glastonbury Goddess Conference, dedicated to Brighid (one of many variations on the name Brigit). It simultaneously combined sparks from several symbolic and magical sources. These were:

- The 2004 Conference flame, ignited from the Sun.
- Brigit's Flame from Kildare.
- The Hiroshima Peace Flame.
- Bridie's Flame from the Hebridian Isle of Lewis.
- The Children's Flame from America.
- The Madonna Ministry Flame from America.

Conference delegates were invited to take home candles they had lit from this. The flame was tended within the Glastonbury Goddess Temple during the following months by priestesses of Avalon, and is now tended by others throughout the world. Priestesses take it in turn to be flame-keepers for the Flame of Avalon and once a month the Glastonbury Goddess Temple becomes the flame-keeper, tending it from dusk to dusk. Everyone who has a Flame of Avalon is invited to join together on these days in global community, sharing the light of the Lady of Avalon.

To find out more, visit goddesstemple.co.uk/flame-of-avalon/

Aphrodite's Flame

This sacred flame was lit in a ritual by priestesses of Aphrodite Elle Hull and Tanisha Rose Jolie during the Full Moon of December 2, 2009. It was inaugurated to be a never-ending source of Aphrodite's love and blessings for anyone who wished to take part, anywhere in the world. In the years that followed, Elle and Tanisha tended Aphrodite's Flame regularly in meditation and ritual. Since 2012, however, Aphrodite's Flame is now perpetually tended by devotees of Aphrodite all over the world.

Elle said:

> Aphrodite's Flame is now a powerful way to invoke the presence of Aphrodite in our hearts, our homes, our temples and spread Her loving energies throughout the world. As others begin to work with Her Flame in meditation, ritual, healing, honouring, sharing, so they, too, will add their energies to the Flame which will see its love and light grow and evolve.

If you want join in holding and working with Aphrodite's Flame, by lighting a candle from one descended from the original Aphrodite's Flame, you can find out how at ellehull.co.uk/aphrodites-flame/

The candles can be used for spells, ritual or meditation as desired – there is no set invocation or ceremony.

Creating New Sacred Flames

In *Wild Earth, Wild Soul*, author Bill Pfeiffer sets out guidelines for a ten-day workshop on environmental awareness, which he calls Wild Earth Intensives (WEI). One of the activities involved is to keep a candle alight for the entire duration of the course. In the book, Bill said:

> One way to make our gratitude tangible is by lighting an 'eternal flame' that will burn continuously for the ten days of the WEI. Depending on site conditions and facilitator skills and preferences, this can be as simple as lighting a candle (and replacing it when it burns down, lighting the next candle from its flame) or as elaborate as starting a 'tipi-style fire' with

a bow drill or similar primitive fire-making method. In both cases, the honouring intent during the lighting and the commitment to keep the fire going are what is most important.

This way of showing gratitude, honour and intent can be used in any workshop, conference, vigil or other magical or spiritual event. Light the candle when all attendees have arrived to signify the start of the work to be done. Speak words of intent, then allocate flame-keepers to mind the candle and ensure it stays alight – lighting a new candle from it each time the old one burns low. At the end of the event, words of thanks can be spoken and the candle extinguished. Alternatively, all of those present can be invited to ignite tea-lights from the flame and let them all burn briefly, then take them home to relight and keep the flame of inspiration going.

Candelifera – She Who Bears the Candle

One goddess specifically associated with candles is Candelifera, a Roman deity with the epithet: 'She who bears the candle'. She is thought to have been the deity thanked for providing artificial light when pregnant women were going through labour. She particularly looked over first-time mothers, who were considered more likely to have a long labour, meaning at least part of the birthing process would take place at night. According to Greek historian Plutarch, the light symbolises birth itself, but the candle may have been considered less of a symbol than an actual kindling of life or even a magic equivalent to the life of the baby. Candelifera is also associated with nursery lights kept burning to ward off spirits of darkness – like the night-light I mentioned kept my own nightmares at bay when I was a child.

As well as asking Candelifera to watch over children and mothers-to-be, you can also honour her if you are doing candle magic, to watch over the birth of your intent as you cast your spell.

Three

Meditation, Divination and Psychic Sight

Meditation

Candles are lovely aids to meditation. Pretty much whatever type of meditation you choose to do, the gentle light of a candle provides the right atmosphere.

You can use the flame itself as the focus for meditation. As with most types of meditation, you need to be in a restful position – seated on the floor, a cushion or a chair. Make sure the candle is positioned at eye height and is securely in its holder. Light the candle, take a few deep breaths in and out, then focus on the flame.

Rachel Patterson, in *Pagan Portals: Meditation*, offers one type of visualisation to do while performing a candle meditation:

> As you breathe in, visualise you are breathing in a pure white cleansing light that fills your body; as you breathe out, visualise all the stresses and worries leaving your body. Do this several times until you start to feel calm and at ease.

Here is another method of candle meditation:

> Sit in front of the candle with your eyes open comfortably (not straining to stare too hard). Let the flame fill your consciousness. It can help to slightly lower your eyelids and defocus your eyes, but do what is comfortable. As you meditate, pay gentle attention to the different parts of the flame.
>
> Candle flames are formed because wax vaporises as it burns. The flame has three zones. The innermost area directly above the wick contains vaporised wax that has not yet burnt. It is the darkest zone. The middle area is yellow and luminous, partly but not entirely burnt, because there is not enough oxygen there to burn away all of the vapour. This is

hotter than the innermost zone, but cooler than the outer area. The outer zone is the hottest. The wax vapour is completely combusted. It is a light blue in colour, but not normally visible.

As you meditate, become aware of these three zones – particularly the outer zone, which is the hardest to see. Let your awareness move between these zones and try not to let your attention wander or your thoughts drift off to other things. If they do, gently guide your attention back to the candle flame.

When you are ready to end the meditation, again take three deep breaths, then extinguish the candle before getting up.

This candle meditation is good preparation for scrying using a candle flame and using a candle flame to increase your psychic sight.

Divination and Oracles

Flames and Smoke

Pyromancy is the ancient magical art of divination by fire. It is one of the earliest forms of divination, probably practised soon after man first discovered how to set light to things. One can imagine shamans staring into the flames and glowing embers of the fires that warmed our Palaeolithic ancestors, foretelling a good hunt or how well the tribe would fare through winter.

In Classical Greece, virgins at the Temple of Athena in Athens used pyromancy and followers of Hephaestus, Greek God of Fire, or his Roman equivalent, Vulcan, probably did too. In Renaissance times pyromancy was a forbidden art along with necromancy, geomancy, aeromancy, hydromancy, chiromancy and spatulamancy (divination using an animal's shoulder blade if you were wondering).

The most basic form of pyromancy involves staring into a fire to watch for patterns and shapes that form in the flames. The magical art is in interpreting what these mean. In modern homes without real fireplaces it is usually easier and safer to watch a candle burn. Divination by candle flame is sometimes called lychnomancy from the Latin 'lychus' meaning 'light'.

- A bright, steady flame is considered a good omen.
- If it burns low and dim, the future could be tough.
- One that goes out is bad and indicates some sort of ending.
- A flame that flickers and flutters indicates there are forces acting against you, uncertainty is holding you back, or you might struggle to get what you desire.
- A twisting flame warns you to beware of treachery or unscrupulous people.
- A spark means an important message will be heading your way.

- If a candle burns much more strongly than you expect, is hotter, brighter or burns down extremely fast, you can expect something extraordinary to happen. It might even indicate your wishes will come true in the most unexpectedly good way. Do be careful, because a sudden rise to success can sometimes then be followed by a crash.

Of course, there can be perfectly rational explanations for candles and flames behaving in certain ways. All candles flicker in a wind, burn more slowly in cold weather and burn faster in hot rooms. A wick that is too small for the size of candle will naturally burn with a slow, low flame, while a wick that is too thick for the width of wax will burn extra fast.

A variation on pyromancy is capnomancy, or divination by smoke. Thin smoke that rises straight upwards is a good sign; smoke that wavers, drifts or billows is a bad omen.

Scrying

Scrying takes divination with candles a step further. Rather than just interpreting the way the flame burns in terms of good or bad omens, this involves using clairvoyance to do a reading with the flame itself. To do this, relax, take a few deep breaths and spend some time staring into the flame with half-closed eyes and see if any shapes or images appear. If you have a specific question you wish answered, think about that, otherwise try to just empty your mind and watch the flame. You might need to wait some time for anything to happen – at least at first. Do you see shapes? Do they remind you of anything? People or objects perhaps? Even if you don't see images in the flame, you might find images come into your mind's eye.

If scrying directly into a flame doesn't work for you, try using a candle beside a bowl of water. Fill a dark-coloured bowl with water then sit in a room lit by a single candle – switch the lights off, close the curtains and position a candle so its light just falls on the surface of the water. Peer into the water with your eyes half closed and see if any shapes or images appear.

When you are finished, jot down everything from the reading in a notebook. You might then need to work out what the images mean, as they are often dim shapes rather than photographic-quality pictures. It is best if you consider what the images mean to you personally rather than immediately look them up in a dictionary of symbols, but if you are stuck you can use books on dream interpretation or tea-leaf reading to help, as the images seen in scrying work in a similar way to those other forms of divination.

If you want to use a crystal ball or a dark mirror, the principles of scrying by candlelight are much the same – although a bowl of water is much cheaper than either of these items.

Using a Candle to Increase Psychic Sight

Earlier in this book I described how to use a candle to cast a circle. If you are visualising light forming a circle of protection, you don't need to actually see the magical energy for it to be effective. Some witches do, but most struggle to see it when they first start learning their craft.

The way I was taught to see magical energy was using the flame of a candle. You need a lit candle and a wand. Start with the candle meditation visualisation I described earlier in which you observe the three parts of the flame. Once you have managed to see the outer part of the flame, pick up a wand or athame and try drawing that outer energy away from the candle with the tip. Don't actually stick a wooden wand into the flame – that would be dangerous and you might end up setting fire to it – get the tip just outside the outer zone of light. Keep your eyes focused on that zone of light and see it being drawn away as energy, a line of light or perhaps a smoky haze. If you like, you can draw a circle of protection all around yourself with the energy.

The trick to doing this is not to be too self-critical. If you keep telling yourself it isn't possible, then you probably won't manage it. It's a bit like when Yoda tells Luke Skywalker in Return of the Jedi: 'Do or don't do. There is no try.'

Once you have your eye in and can see this energy, practise using the same psychic sight when looking at people. You might be able to see the same kind of glow around them that you can around the candle – that is one of the first steps towards learning to psychically view people's auras or etheric bodies.

Note that magical energy is not the same thing as the light in the outer zone of a candle. They are different things entirely, and magical energy isn't measurable by scientific processes as far as I am aware, they just look similar in psychic sight and so the candle flame is a useful tool to get your psychic eyes working.

However, I do wonder if it is our innate awareness of how close to magic a candle's flame appears that is the reason so many people naturally find candles magical.

Four

Chandlery, Safety and History

Chandlery

Chandlery is the word for candle making. I don't have space in this book to go into candle making in much depth, but I do recommend trying it. Candles you have made yourself are far better for magical work than ones bought in a shop. Here are two methods of making your own candles.

Rolled Beeswax Spell Candles

These are very easy to make. You need a sheet of beeswax and a wick suitable for a small candle. These can be bought over the internet or at crafting shops. Cut the sheet in quarters. One quarter will make one small spell candle.

Place the wick along one edge of the beeswax quarter, with enough sticking out of one end so that you will be able to light the candle. Warm the sheet slightly with a hairdryer so it is a little flexible, then carefully and firmly roll it up so the wick is in the middle. Press the outside edge down so it stays in place. Trim it with your boline knife if necessary. Pinch a tiny bit of wax around the end of the wick to prime it if it isn't already wax coated. *Voilà,* one spell candle.

Recycled Container Candle

Gather up all your candle stubs and bits of wax clinging to candle holders, plus a container that once held a candle.

You will need to buy a new pre-stiffened wick with a small metal disc at the bottom (a sustainer).

The old wax will need to be melted. Don't put it into a pan that goes straight onto the cooker, use a double-boiler or place a basin inside a pan of boiling water. If your wax was previously part of a spell candle, to dispel the old magic stir it three times widdershins while it is melting and say:

I dispel all influences on this wax. Be gone, be gone, be gone.

When the wax has all melted, dip the end of the wick with the sustainer into the wax just to coat it, then pop it into the container and let the wax stick it to the bottom.

Then carefully pour the rest of the melted wax in around the wick. If it is a tall container you will need to place a pencil or something across the top and prop the wick against it to stop it from listing to one side. Leave the candle somewhere to cool down and set – the fridge is ideal.

Trim the wick to a centimetre or two before lighting the candle.

Candle Safety

However magical candles might be, they are dangerous and you should always take care when using them. Below is some sensible candle safety advice offered by the UK Fire Service:

- Always put candles on a heat resistant surface. Be especially careful with night-lights and tea-lights, which get hot enough to melt plastic.
- Put them in a proper holder. Candles need to be held firmly upright by the holder so they won't fall over. The holder needs to be stable too.
- Don't put candles near curtains or other fabrics – or furniture.
- Keep them out of draughts.
- Don't put them under shelves. It's easy to forget that there's a lot of heat above a burning candle. If you put it under a shelf or other surface then it can ignite the underside and lead to a fire. Make sure there's at least one metre between a candle and any surface above it.
- Keep clothes and hair away. If there's any chance you could lean across a candle and forget it's there, put it somewhere else. You don't want to set fire to your clothes or your hair.
- Candles should be out of reach of children and pets.
- Keep candles apart. Ideally leave at least 10cm between two burning candles.
- Take care with scented candles. These turn to liquid to release their fragrance, so put them in a glass or metal holder if they aren't already in a container.
- Extinguish candles before moving them. Also, don't let anything fall into the hot wax, such as match sticks.
- Don't leave them burning. Extinguish candles before you

leave a room. Never go to sleep with a candle still burning. And never leave a burning candle or oil burner in a child's bedroom.

- Use a snuffer or a spoon to put them out. It's safer than blowing them, which can send sparks and hot wax flying.
- Double-check they're out. Candles that have been put out can go on smouldering and start a fire. Make sure they're completely out.

I know that some candle spells and rituals go against the advice given above, particularly in regard to moving candles. What I would say is, if you do move candles, make sure they are in candleholders designed for being moved and are very securely in place. Have a suitable procedure in mind in case of accidents, such as a fire blanket or extinguisher.

Artificial Candles

While real candles are always preferable to artificial ones in my opinion, there are times when it just isn't safe or practical to use the genuine item. If health and safety regulations forbid them, you need to leave the lights unattended or there are likely to be young children around, it is much better to avoid mishap.

The kinds of large artificial candles I prefer to use if possible are those that come with a real wax shell and a small electric light inside. They look very much like the real thing and are at least partly made of wax. I cleanse and consecrate these in the same way as a real candle before first using them, then charge them magically in the light of a real candle before putting them to use. (Be careful not to melt them though.)

For smaller candles, artificial tea-lights designed to flicker in a natural way can be popped inside coloured glass containers and look pretty convincing at a casual glance.

History of Candle Making

I left the boring bit to last – history. Okay, history isn't necessarily boring, but I don't think it is as interesting as actually doing spells. Nevertheless, having an overview of the history of candles can help get the magic into context.

Candle making developed independently in many parts of the world at different times. The Romans began making dipped candles from tallow around 500BCE, although they mainly used lamps filled with olive oil. Romans often gave candles to each other as gifts during Saturnalia, a winter festival similar to Yule or Christmas. The Chinese made candles from whale fat during the Qin Dynasty (221–206BCE). In India, wax from boiling cinnamon was used for temple candles from very early times.

Interestingly, early Christians disapproved of candles for use in worship. They considered them heathen because they were frequently used in Pagan rites. Obviously, they got over this aversion quite quickly.

In Europe, candles became the most common form of lighting during the Middle Ages. Candles then were primarily made from tallow or beeswax. Tallow is extracted from the suet of sheep and cattle. It stinks, but was cheap so was what most ordinary people used, replacing or supplementing reed-lights. Beeswax, which smells lovely but has always been expensive, was used for church candles. The Christian festivals of Candlemas, on February 2, and the feast of Saint Lucy, on December 13, became very popular. Both are candle festivals, with candles being blessed at Candlemas and St Lucy's Day being a festival of light close to the Winter Solstice. However, there are suggestions that both of these feast days may have older, Pagan origins.

In the 18th century, whale oil (spermaceti) began to be commonly used for candle making. In the mid 19th century that was superseded by paraffin wax. Stearin – purified animal fat that doesn't smell horrible – was also developed and often added to paraffin wax to harden it. Recently, vegetable waxes including soya have become popular for making candles, although actually the first American colonists discovered that wax from bayberries could be used in chandlery.

The use of candles for general lighting waned when electric lights were developed, but for mood and magic they are showing no sign of dying out.

Candles in Witchcraft History

Candles became a common component for witchcraft, spellwork and divination in Europe from the Middle Ages. An 11th century treatise, *Lots of the Twelve Patriarchs*, described a method of predicting the future that involved fasting by the light of 'a candle of double weight' for two days.

When Alice Kyter was accused of murdering her husband by sorcery in the 12th century, according to PG Maxwell-Stuart in *The British Witch – The Biography*, one of the accusations levelled against her was that she had used dead people's nails, buttock-hairs and the clothes of children who had died before they could be baptised as ingredients in candles employed for maleficent purposes.

Another example given in *The British Witch* is Joan 'alias Ward', cited to come before a court on June 10 and 11, 1490:

> Here...we are given an example of the kind of thing she did. She would measure a man's height, have a wax candle made the same length, and then have it offered in front of a statue or painting (*coram imagine*). Once it was lit, the man would waste away just as the candle did.

Any history of candle magic has to include the infamous Hand of Glory. Documents from the 18th century describe this as the pickled hand of a hanged man combined with a candle made from the corpse's fat, which was supposed to have the power of rendering motionless those who fell within its light. A Hand of Glory is on display in the Whitby Museum, in Yorkshire, if you feel like seeing one.

References and Bibliography

Books

A Kitchen Witch's World of Magical Herbs and Plants by Rachel Patterson, Moon Books

Aromatherapy and Essential Oils for Beginners by Kimberly Jones, Adish Books

Candle Burning Rituals by Marie Bruce, quantum

Element Encyclopedia of 5000 Spells by Judika Illes, Harper Element

Grimoire of a Kitchen Witch by Rachel Patterson, Moon Books

Magical Candle Crafting by Ember Grant, Llewellyn Worldwide

Magic Crystals, Sacred Stones by Mélusine Draco, Axis Mundi

Pagan Portals – Irish Paganism by Morgan Daimler, Moon Books,

Pagan Portals – Meditation by Rachel Patterson, Moon Books,

Pagan Portals – Hoodoo by Rachel Patterson, Moon Books

Practical Candle Burning: Spells and Rituals for Every Purpose by Raymond Buckland, Llewellyn's Practical Magick

Spells and Rituals Using Candle Magic by Sally Love, Caxton Editions

The Book of Practical Candle Magic by Leo Vinci, Aquarian Press

The British Witch – The Biography by PG Maxwell-Stuart, Amberley Publishing

The New Candle Book by Gloria Nicol, Lorenz Books

Wild Earth, Wild Soul by Bill Pfeiffer, Moon Books

Websites

www.badwitch.co.uk

goddesstemple.co.uk/flame-of-avalon/

ellehull.co.uk/aphrodites-flame/

www.thewhitegoddess.co.uk/

www.witchipedia.com/

www.candlemakers.co.uk/

www.fireservice.co.uk/safety/candles

About the Author

Lucya Starza is an eclectic witch living in London, England, in a rambling old house with her husband and cat. She is a Gardnerian Wiccan, but first trained in witchcraft with Shan at House of the Goddess. She also attends an OBOD druidic seedgroup and loves to get together with friends for tea, magic and cackling. Her previous writing includes contributions to the Moon Books publications *Naming the Goddess, Essays in Contemporary Paganism* and *Paganism 101* and she regularly blogs at www.badwitch.co.uk.

Moon Books invites you to begin or deepen your encounter with Paganism, in all its rich, creative, flourishing forms.

Candle magic is something almost everyone has tried. Who hasn't made a wish over a birthday cake? Candle spells are among the easiest yet also the most effective to perform. They are perfect for anyone who wants to have a go at casting a spell for the first time and for the solitary witch with a busy life. Yet candles are also an important part of modern Pagan witchcraft rituals. They are used to mark the quarters of the circle, they are placed on the altar and can represent the changing seasons of the year. This book is aimed at all who want to use candle magic, from beginners to those experienced in the Craft; with everything from simple castings to elaborate and beautiful ceremonies. It offers spells, rituals, seasonal celebrations, divination techniques, meditations, a guide to sacred flames, ways to make your own candles, a look at the history of candles, and more.

"...a 'must-have' introduction to the fascinating subject of candle magic..."
Melusine Draco, Principal of Coven of the Scales and
author of the Traditional Witchcraft series of books

"...It has quickly become my preferred book for all aspects of candle magic."
Philip Heselton, author of Wiccan Roots: Gerald Gardner
and the Modern Witchcraft Revival

"...An immensely useful book for anyone interested in candle magic or spell work...
joining the select few 'well thumbed' volumes on my shelf that I refer back to
again and again."
Mabh Savage, author of A Modern Celt: Seeking the Ancestors

LUCYA STARZA is an eclectic witch living in London, England, in a rambling old house with her husband and cat. She writes A Bad Witches Blog at **www.badwitch.co.uk** and has contributed to *Naming the Goddess*, *Essays in Contemporary Paganism* and *Paganism 101*.

MIND, BODY & SPIRIT
UK £9.99
US $12.95

Cover image: Lucya Starza
Cover design by Design Deluxe
www.moon-books.net

US $12.95
ISBN 978-1-78535-043-6

9 781785 350436

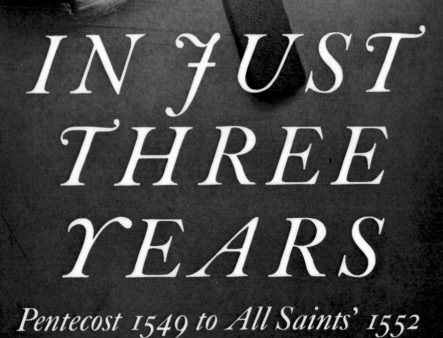

IN JUST THREE YEARS

Pentecost 1549 to All Saints' 1552

❧ A Tale of Two Prayer Books ❧

CANON DAVID JENNINGS